LIFE CHANG

LIFE CHANGERS

NARRATIVES OF A RECENT MOVEMENT
IN THE SPIRIT OF PERSONAL RELIGION

By

HAROLD BEGBIE

Author of " Broken Earthenware "

Nor will that day dawn at a human nod
When, bursting through the network superpos'd
By selfish occupation—plot and plan,
Lust, avarice, envy—liberated man,
All difference with his fellow man compos'd,
Shall be left standing face to face with God.

—MATTHEW ARNOLD

Thirty-sixth Thousand

PREFACE

QUIETLY and unobtrusively, an interesting work has been going on for the last four or five years among the undergraduates of many Universities, not only here in England but all over the world. This work, by its own development, has attracted the attention of the religious authorities of many countries, and largely originated from the activity of a single person.

Some years ago I made the acquaintance of this man, and learned from him that he considers privacy essential to his method, at any rate that he regards publicity as a grave danger. His genius, I think, lies in thinking with an intense preoccupation of individual persons. To him the man is much more than the multitude, which is probably true in the spiritual sphere. Any idea of "mass production" in his work is to him dreadfully repellent. Therefore it is that he shuns publicity of any kind, and never for one moment dreams of calculating his gains in statistics.

For a particular reason I was greatly interested in the work of this unusual teacher. I found that he was able to do, quite quietly, rationally, and unconventionally, a work among the educated and the refined which hitherto I had chiefly associated with a more exciting propaganda directed to the broken earthenware of our discordant civilisations. I discovered that he could change the very life of students and scholars in the course of conversation, change that life as profoundly and persuasively as ever I have known it changed by devoted missionaries among the ignorant and base. Further, I discovered that his method was distinguished by a single characteristic, which struck me at once as going to the very heart and soul of all religious difficulties.

We became friends ; we corresponded with each other ; at intervals we met and discussed the progress of his work. Then, in the summer of the year 1922, I accepted an invitation to meet a number of University men from both sides of the Atlantic who were to gather together in a house-party for the purpose of discussing spiritual experience and the best means of privately extending this remarkable work of personal religion.

Those memorable days began, so far as I was concerned, with disappointment, even with disapproval. I did not like the manner in which the early discussions were conducted ; many of the phrases used in describing a really unique religious experience seemed to me second-hand and unconvincing ; I could not help feeling that I was not merely wasting my time, but that I was foolishly permitting my nerves to be unprofitably irritated.

Some of the younger men consulted me in private as to my opinion of their leader and his method of conducting these house-parties. I told them of my disappointment and disapproval. The first consequence of this confession on my part was a tendency to a cave ; I found myself a rallying-point for discontent and mutiny. But this danger was averted by the extreme frankness and modesty of the remarkable man who had brought us together. He changed the manner of the public discussions, and left me more leisure to cultivate in private conversation a real acquaintance with my fellow-guests. From that moment every hour of my visit became interesting to a degree which truly one cannot well exaggerate.

The character of these men, some of them so brilliant in scholarship, others so splendid in athletics, and all of them, without one exception, so modest and so disturbingly honest, was responsible for my reawakened interest. They were men of the first-class, men whom one may fairly call not only the fine flower of our English-speaking civilisation, but representative of the best hope we possess of weathering the storms of materialism which so palpably threaten to overwhelm the ship which carries the spiritual fortunes of humanity. It was impossible in their company to doubt any longer that the man who had changed their lives, and had made them also changers of other men's lives, was a person of very considerable importance. One regarded him with a new interest, a fresh reverence.

Yet—and this was perhaps the thought which most influenced me in those first moments of hesitation—some of these men spoke to me with troubled criticism of their leader, disliking some of his pet phrases, disapproving as vigorously as I did of his theological opinions, but all sticking to him with an unconquerable loyalty as the man who had worked a great miracle in their lives, and who was by far the most remarkable man of their experience in spite of everything that troubled either their taste or their judgment.

Among these men was a young officer who had not yet undergone a spiritual change, and who carried about with him, behind a charming social appearance, a soul that was haunted to the point of torture by his past. I walked often with this man in the beautiful gardens surrounding the house, and he told me a number of extremely moving stories of his experiences, first as a pilot in the war, and afterwards as a trainer of pilots. He could not bear to think of the dead boys whom he had passed as fit to fly—many of them killed in their first or second flight. But every now and then he would turn from the war to speak of F. B., the leader, expressing an anxious doubt as to whether even this miracle-worker could ever save him from an intolerable depression of the soul.

This doubt was uttered in no dismal or tragical manner, but with a smile very boyish and agreeable, and in a tone which rather suggested that he looked forward to his first private talk with F. B. as little more than a curious experience. He smoked many cigarettes in a rather feverish fashion as he spoke to me of " something on his mind," and I noticed that though the smile seldom left his face his hands trembled, and there was always a distracted look in his eyes.

On the last night of the house-party, the young soldier went to see F. B. alone, just before ten o'clock. When the rest of us went to bed, towards midnight, that consultation was still going on. Next morning, as I was entering the dining-room, I felt my arm touched from behind, and, turning about, found this man closing up to my side, his pale face and suffering eyes lighted by a strange smile of boyish gladness and triumphant serenity, in spite of all the marks of a sleepless night and great spiritual strain which showed behind the brightness of his face like so many bruises.

He asked me to go with him into the garden for a moment, and there he told me that he had been with F. B. till past two in the morning, that he had confessed everything, that (laughing quietly) a most extraordinary change had taken place inside him, that he was no longer oppressed, that he was indeed amazingly happy, and, best thing of all, he now had a definite work before him. F. B. said, he told me on a deeper note, that he must cross the sea to a far country, that he must there seek out a youth whom he had once put on the wrong road of life, that he must adopt that youth, bring him back to England watch over him, and never leave him till his soul was right.

The profound happiness of this man, and his deep joy in the hard and difficult task which he had most gladly undertaken, made so great an impression upon me that I presently sought out F. B. and told him of my wish to write this book. I said that a book which faithfully described such wonderful work might do something to create in the minds of many people a new and intelligent interest in religion ; that religion was losing ground and materialism was gaining ground chiefly because the power of religion to change the lives of men was now almost wholly unknown, or, if known, was regarded as an example of mere emotionalism working on weak intellects.

He agreed with this contention, stipulating only that no mention of his name should be made in the book ; he left me free to conclude my own arrangements with those of my fellow-guests who seemed most likely to further the purpose in my mind.

In this manner the pages which follow came to be written.

CONTENTS

LIFE CHANGERS

CHAPTER I

ACCORDING TO THY FAITH

At the outset I will make it quite plain how the method of F. B. chiefly differs, in my opinion, from the methods of most other men engaged in work of this nature.

But I must be frank with the reader, and tell him at once that F. B. would probably correct me at almost every point of my explanation, thrusting in with theological formulas which he himself considers essential to the success of his work.

I make bold to think, however, on the same ground which entitles the least of us to say that the onlooker sees most of the game, that I discern better than F. B. himself what makes his work so extraordinarily fruitful. This would be an insufferably vain assumption if I had not confirmed my opinion on several occasions in discourse with those whose lives have been so marvellously changed under the influence of F. B. They are my witnesses. In the third chapter of this book the reader will see how amply I am justified in proffering this particular excuse for what otherwise would certainly be an impertinent presumption.

When a man who has heard of F. B., or has met him in a fellow-undergraduate's room, goes to see F. B. in private, he usually begins by a statement of his theological difficulties.

F. B. hears him out. He never interrupts. He waits patiently and quite unemotionally, his eyes sympathetically studying his visitor, until the young man's mind has emptied itself of all its intellectual objections to Christianity—those grave intellectual objections which distract so many minds, and which so few Christian apologists ever face with the uncompromising honesty taken for granted among men of science.

His methods of approach vary with each individual. He may spend six months making friends with one man without any reference to his personal needs ; or, even earlier, he may make some such remark as this : " It isn't any intellectual difficulty which is keeping you from God. It is sin." In all instances his approach is marked by friendliness and sympathetic insight. The difficulty may be anything from the worst and most deadly sin to a bad habit reckoned by some people to be comparatively harmless. The cure is always the same.

In nine cases out of ten the diagnosis is true, for his wide experience with a sin-sick world has made him a master in what some call " soul-surgery." But the correctness of diagnosis is not the only point. What matters much more is this, that he interprets the symptoms of a distressed spirit and reveals the real cause. It is sin, a sin which it refuses to give up, does not want to give up, and will not give up without a tremendous struggle, which is locking the door on its natural peace, its natural happiness, and its natural power.

The theory on which he works may be expressed in simple language after this manner :

Sin is a word which denotes a choosing. The will chooses the bad. It is its duty, in the interest of the world, to choose the good. It is fatal to its own peace and happiness to choose the bad. But it chooses the bad. This act of choosing constitutes the sin.

So long as it consents to the slavery of the bad it cannot perceive that to choose good is not only right, but a matter of the first importance to its own liberty. All sin is reaction ; it is an attempt on the part of the human will to reverse the processes of growth—-to go back, not to go forward ; to descend, not to ascend. The will which chooses the bad, therefore, is in opposition to the will of the universe, that is to say, the Divine Will, the Will of God immanent in growth.

In order to be free from the tyranny of sin, and in order to gain the natural liberty of a will in harmony with the will of the universe, there must be, first and foremost, a *desire* for the good. Without that desire the will is powerless. But let that desire exist, however feebly or intermittently, and the enslaved will is neither helpless nor hopeless. Let that desire become the strongest and intensest longing of the heart, and not only can the will be delivered from its oppression, but a change of the will can be brought about so complete, so pervasive of the whole being, so creative in power and goodness, that it may truly be described as a new birth of the soul.

No man can sound the depths of his own natural peace, or rise to the heights of his own natural bliss, who is not conscious of the presence and the companionship of God. This consciousness is natural to the soul whose will is in harmony with the will of God, but it is impossible to the soul whose will is not converted to the divine will. The work of religion is to create a longing for good in the soul of man, so that it may escape from the slavery of sins fatal to its own peace, and reach its highest usefulness to the purposes of development in a direct and living consciousness of God.

Consciousness of God, he holds, is the natural state of things. Sin is unnatural, and prevents the natural state of things from obtaining. Sin is unnatural in the sense that it is the will of the creature opposing itself to the will of the Creator. Always it is sin, and only it is sin, which blinds the eyes and hardens the heart of mankind. It may be the smallest of sins, one of those sins which we describe as merely amiable weaknesses ; but let it be in charge of a soul and directing its course, let it be a sin which we find ourselves unable to give up, which we recognise as unworthy, and yet cling to, and we are living in the cold, we are moving in the shadows, and all our faculties are in gyves.

I think this point of view helps one to understand how it is that many people who profess religious beliefs, and even devote themselves to religious work, are often so unattractive, so entirely lacking, not only in power, but in charm.

It would seem that the whole matter turns upon a

complete unison of the two wills, the divine and the human. They must both want the same things to happen, they must both desire the same qualities, they must both be pursuing the same end. Discordance between the will of the creature and the will of its Creator results in a weakening of the consciousness of God in the heart of the creature. Men may live very religiously and yet fail to dislodge their will from some form of selfishness which is fatal to their possession by the grace of God. They may be perfectly pure, and yet vain ; or wonderfully generous with their time and money, yet intolerantly wedded to their own ideas ; or they may lay down their lives for their religion, and yet never have loved anybody so well as themselves.

Perfectly to realise the divine companionship seems to depend solely and exclusively on one act of the will, an act which denies all the values of the animal senses, and embraces, not only with an absolute and unquestioning surrender, but with a profound love and an ardent craving for satisfaction, the will of its Creator. Hence at the very threshold of the spiritual life one is confronted by the challenge of love. No one can proceed far on that immortal journey who does not perfectly and most earnestly hunger and thirst after the divine excellence, who does not long for perfection, and who does not wish with all his heart to be rid of every selfishness which disfigures character and impoverishes spiritual power.

It is a hard challenge, but there it is ; and one must agree that the universe itself is hard. There is not much discernible softness in the laws of Nature.

Spiritual laws are no less exacting, so far as one can see, than the laws which appear to govern the material universe. Perhaps the attribution to the Deity of a softness, a vacillation, and a sentimentalism which would be contemptible in a man, has done far more to weaken in humanity the sense of the moral law than the earlier attribution to Him of such miserable bad qualities as jealousy, vindictiveness, and a gross partiality.

Moreover, if we are quite honest and rational, must we not agree that this spiritual law is just ? And if it is that, who shall bring a charge against it ? History is the chronicle of an ascent on the part of man from unquestioning animalism to a disturbed moral consciousness. Each step has been made by the deliberate choice of man between good and evil. No one has told him what is good. No hand has guided him from what is evil. First for his own safety, and afterwards out of loyalty to the past and desire for a nobler future, he has chosen good and rejected evil. Further, with each difficult ascent he has heightened the demands of good and widened the categories of evil. Each Alp of his toilsome ascent has revealed to him a greater height to be reached, a more difficult peak to be scaled. And the greatest of the sons of men, those who have carried the human race on their shoulders, have not complained that thus it should be.

Without this deliberate and unaided election for good it is difficult to perceive how any honourable progress could have been made in the life of the human race. And if our ancestors made that election, and if they opposed themselves to all the

gross forces of materialism in the earliest and
roughest ages of the human epic, are we now to
complain, we whose lot has been rendered comparatively so easy by their heroic endurance, that it is a
hard thing to expect us to choose good rather than
evil, to give our wills to rightness and not to wrong-
ness, to excellence and not to imperfection ?

The reader must bear in mind that we are not now
thinking in any way of rewards and punishments.
The idea of heaven and hell does not at present enter
into our thoughts. We are discussing simply the
question of individual human progress here upon
earth. We are asking ourselves, " How can a man
ascend from brutality to humanity, from weakness
to power, from unrest to serenity ? " The struggle
is a hard one, as each man knows for himself, save
only those whose souls are doped by the swill in
the trough of animalism. In order to render that
struggle intelligible, and therefore less difficult, we
are endeavouring, in the spirit of men of science
examining the physical laws of the material universe,
to discover the spiritual laws of the universe of
reality.

In this inquiry we find from the history of mankind
that ascent is the consequence of desire   The
greatest of all human words, because it denotes the
greatest of human powers, is the word love—a word
which signifies desire at its highest intensity. What
a man loves with all his will he finds it easy to obtain ;
the struggle entailed in getting what we want can be
measured, and is absolutely determined, by the
quality of our desire. There is no injustice in the
condition, " According to thy faith be it done unto

thee." That condition represents, indeed, man's idea of perfect fairness. To hunger and thirst after a virtue rightly commands that virtue; half-heartedly to wish for a virtue rightly brings only a fragment of that virtue into our possession. To obtain a living and creating consciousness of the divine companionship our wills must desire that blessing to the extremest intensity of love, certainly to the total exclusion of our own petty wishes.

M. Coué confirms the teaching of Dr. Milne Bramwell, who told me nearly twenty years ago that auto-suggestion can do nothing without desire on the part of the patient. M. Coué tells me that his patients cure themselves by believing in the possibility of their cures, and that this belief is strong or weak according to their wish for healing. Many people afflicted with even painful diseases do not really desire to be cured of them—wherein we may see a spiritual parable. In any case, neither hypnotism nor auto-suggestion can give to the mind a notion which it does not possess; in each instance desire or tendency must be there, and all that hypnotism or auto-suggestion can do is to stimulate that desire, to strengthen that tendency. " According to thy faith be it done unto thee."

Christ enters into all these conversions. It is He who inspires the work. It is He who authorises the teaching. It is He who encourages the seeker to believe and the abandoned to hope.

In all this Christ is manifest. For not only is the teaching His teaching, but in Him as in no other being who has ever lifted up the face of man from the dust we behold the Will of God, the divine Will which has brought creation into existence and set in motion the laws of the spiritual universe. He personifies for us the inconceivable, the unimaginable, the infinite. He humanises the superhuman. He leads us so convincingly out of the delusions of the visible and so confidently into the realities of the invisible that truly we can say of Him, He came from God.

The testimony of those who have been changed by conversion and themselves have become changers of human life, whatever their various theological inheritance, is, that any form of wilfulness in the mind is a vital bar to a vital consciousness of God ; that as soon as the mind, with real honesty and a consuming desire for that divine consciousness, hates its sin and turns to God, the will is new born ; and, finally, that henceforth life for them becomes transfigured by a joy of which they had hitherto no conception, a joy which seems to consist of, first, a poignant conviction of the reality of God's response to their craving ; second, an entire sense of freedom from a division in personality ; and third, a sense of creative power in the lives of other men, making for a like happiness with their own.

Ruskin used to say that he did not wonder at what men suffered, but at what they lost. The idea that immortality is something to be attained by the purified human will hungering and thirsting after the perfection of God helps one to realise the tremendous significance of Christ's question, " For what shall it profit a man if he shall gain the whole world, and lose his own soul ? "

Also it helps one, I think, to see a depth of meaning in that familiar phrase—too familiar, perhaps—*The Peace of God.*

Therefore, with what impatience, and with how despairing a regret, must those who long for the Peace of God see the Churches wasting their energies on matters which divide rather than unite, neglecting, for teachings which obscure, depress, and after two thousand years of repetition make no difference to man or nation, the one great central teaching of their Master which saves the individual and glorifies the human race ?

The future of civilisation, rising at this moment from the ruins of materialism, would seem to lie in an intelligent use by man of this ultimate source of spiritual Power. To make use of that Power it appears necessary that the human will must be sounding the same note, pursuing the same end, working in the same spirit. One of the simplest sayings of Jesus makes it clear that man's ability to draw upon this inexhaustible and immeasurable source of eternal life is determined by his desire for it : " Blessed are they which do hunger and thirst after righteousness ; for they shall be filled."

With this understood, one can proceed to the narratives ; but I would leave in the mind of the reader as a final word on the method of F. B. that the distinguishing characteristic of his work is the exclusive and pathological emphasis he lays on the power of sin to rob a man's soul of its natural health —sin being understood, not merely as great vices, but as any motion in the will contrary to such excellence as that soul might reach by a genuine desire for spiritual growth.

This brief attempt to explain in untheological language the lines on which my friend works his miracles of conversion may help the reader, I hope, to enter with a quicker sympathy and a more rational understanding into the narratives which follow.

CHAPTER II

THE SOUL SURGEON

As I have already hinted, the impressive thing in
F. B. is that a man so unimpressive can work miracles
—miracles which would seem to demand extraordinary
qualities of mind. He helps one to believe that truth
may yet be an even greater force in human affairs
than personality.

In appearance he is a young-looking man of middle
life, tall, upright, stoutish, clean-shaven, spectacled,
with that mien of scrupulous, shampooed, and
almost medical cleanness, or freshness, which is so
characteristic of the hygienic American.
His carriage and his gestures are distinguished
by an invariable alertness. He never droops, he
never slouches. You find him in the small hours of
the morning with the same quickness of eye and the
same athletic erectness of body which seem to bring
a breeze into the breakfast-room. Few men so
quiet and restrained exhale a spirit of such contagious well-being.
A slight American accent marks his speech, and is
perhaps richly noticeable only when he makes use of
American colloquialisms. The voice is low but
vigorous, with a sincere ring of friendliness and good
humour—the same friendliness and good-humour

which are characteristic of his manners. He strikes
one on a first meeting as a warm-hearted and very
happy man, who can never know what it is to be
either physically tired or mentally bored. I am
tempted to think that if Mr. Pickwick had given
birth to a son, and that son had emigrated in boyhood to America, he would have been not unlike this
amiable and friendly surgeon of souls.

Fuller acquaintance with F. B. brings to one's
mind the knowledge that in spite of his boyish
cheerfulness he is of the house and lineage of all true
mystics, from Plotinus to Tolstoy. He attributes,
without question, to the Deity certain motions in
himself which another might well assign to movements of his own unconsciousness. For example, it
is his habit to wake very early from sleep, and to
devote an hour or more to complete silence of soul
and body ; in this silence he is waiting for what he
calls " the promptings of the Holy Spirit," which
come to him, and he thus receives his guidance for
the day—he is to write to one man, he is to call upon
another, and so on. Psychologists would tell him
that those orders proceed from his own unconsciousness, and are the fruit of sleep's mentation, the
harvest of his yesterday's thoughts and solicitudes.
Such an explanation, of course, does not rob these
motions of their spiritual value. But it is an explanation, I think, which may help those whose conception
of the Deity entirely prevents them from believing
either in His interposition or His colloquies with the
human soul. It may help such as these to realise
that a sincere acquiescence in the divine Will may

enable the human will more perfectly to apprehend the spiritual influences of its environment, and to act more concordantly upon the intuitions of its own spirit. Mystery remains ; but it is a mystery which neither detracts from the unimaginable glory of God nor degrades the human spirit to the mechanical level of a gramophone.

The mysticism of F. B. shows itself more normally, and one might almost say more old-fashionedly, in his unquestioning conviction that there is a blessing in reading the Bible (quite apart from the literary blessing of feeding the mind on such beautiful English), and also in his faith that sincere prayer, even for material help, is constantly answered. But his great emphasis, I think, is laid on spiritual silence, and the article of his faith which more than any other seems to give him his unique power is the mystical notion that in every man there is " a piece of divinity " hungering and thirsting for expression, a piece of divinity which best makes its presence felt to the soul in periods of silence.

He sees a significant parable in the scriptural incident of the blind man healed by the touch of Jesus. At the first touch of those gentle fingers the blind saw men walking as trees ; at the second he saw " every man clearly." F. B. tells those who come to him that so long as they see men in the mass, see them as a forest, their spiritual eyes are only half opened ; to see them individually, man by man, and each man a piece of divinity, an heir of eternal life, requires the second touch of the spiritual hand—the miracle of conversion.

One of the phrases he never tires of hammering
into the minds of those who desire to help the progress of men religiously is borrowed, I believe, from
the Japanese : " It's no use throwing eye-medicine
out of a two-storey window." Drop by drop, and
with the utmost precision, the extremest care, the
medicine of God must be directed to the individual
soul. He holds that little good is done by the
extravagant methods of so many religious organisa-
tions to make Christians of men in the mass. He
goes even further than this, with much experience to
justify him, and teaches that numbers of those who
are thus so heroically but vainly striving to Chris-
tianise the multitudes are themselves strangers to the
central power and mystery of the Christian religion.
Let me say at once that no small part of his busy life is
devoted to the conversion of religious teachers, many
of whom continue his fervent and grateful disciples.

How he came by this conviction of the personal
character of religion, this intense conviction which
drives him so earnestly and successfully on his happy
way—for he is a man of extreme happiness—may
appear in the following brief narrative of his life.

He was born in America, and at the age of twenty-
four was ordained into the ministry of the Lutheran
Church. A theological student at his seminary had
accused him of ambition, and to correct any tendency
in that course F. B. chose a most difficult quarter of
Philadelphia for his initial labours. He was moder-
ately successful in his work, but was conscious of
an inner hindrance, a something in himself which
prevented the great message of Christianity from
" getting through." He spent a year in the Near

East, and in 1908 paid a visit to England with the express intention of attending the religious convention at Keswick Here the miracle occurred which so altered his life that ever since he has been able to show a great host of people how they may obtain a like reconstruction.

Weary of himself, but not yet sick of asking what he was, and what he ought to be, this young American one day entered a little village church in Cumberland, under whose humble roof was gathered a congregation of seventeen people. The service was taken by a woman. " My feelings," F. B. has told me, " were very unhappy ; I won't call them despairing ; they were just feelings of great unhappiness. Grudges against certain religious people were there in my mind, fermenting ; I felt that I could justly accuse those men of hard-heartedness, high-handedness, bigotry. They had always seemed to be opposing me—opposing my work. Yet the main cause of my disquiet was the knowledge of my own heart that it was guilty of three things, sticking there like glue, stopping all the free working of the generosity and happiness I longed to experience—selfishness, pride, ill-will. These three things were in my blood—selfishness, pride, ill-will ; I could not get rid of them ; while they were there I knew that the better part of me couldn't function as it ought. Think of it—selfishness, pride, ill-will ; and I called myself a Christian, tried to make other people Christians ! "

The woman preacher spoke of some particular aspect of the cross—he does not now recall precisely what that aspect was, but he says that in some manner for which he cannot account her quite simple words " personalised the Cross," and that while he brooded on this idea in a reverie of mind there came to him, very palpably and with a most poignant realism, albeit with no suddenness, no dramatic intensity, a vision of the Crucified.

He was conscious at once of two shuddering realisations—the realisation of a great abyss between him and the suffering Christ, the realisation of an infinite sorrow in the face of his Master. These realisations dissipated the chaos in his mind. There was now no hesitancy, no feeling of a divided will, no sense of calculation and argument ; a wave of strong emotion, rising up within him from the depths of his estranged spiritual life, seemed, as it were, to lift his soul from its anchorage of selfishness and to bear it across that great sundering abyss to the foot of the Cross. There he made his surrender to the divine Will ; there he lost all sense of oppression and helplessness. It was the work of a moment, and a gesture of his spirit invisible to human eyes.

I asked him to recall if he could the physical sensations of that moment of surrender, so that the reality of his experience might not fade from my mind, in the rather conventional language of revivalism. How would he describe to a doctor what happened to him ? How would he tell that experience to a man who had never heard of Jesus ?

He said, " I remember one sensation very distinctly ; it was a vibrant feeling as if a strong current of life had suddenly been poured into me. That followed on my surrender. No ; it came at the same time. It was instantaneous."

What followed on this sensation, was the dazed feeling of " a great shaking up." He sat for some moments in a certain confusion of mind, not trembling in the body, but conscious of a long vibration in his soul, as though it was still throbbing under the shock of this new experience. There was no immediate feeling of lightness, no rejoicing sense of deliverance and liberation. He was conscious of a very mighty change in himself, but for some time could only think of that change in terms of its physical effects.

He returned to the house at which he was staying, and told at the table of his hostess what had happened to him. He related this experience in simple language, and with no emotion, relating it, however, with the natural pleasure of one who has made an important discovery. There was a Cambridge man staying in the house, and after luncheon this man asked F. B. to go for a walk with him. They walked for some hours round the lake, and it was during this walk that both illumination and relief came to this surgeon of souls. He said, in his explanation to the other, that to keep his sense of the divine his heart must be empty of all sin, of every vestige of his discordant past. There and then he decided to write six letters to those men in America against whom he had long borne a justifiable grudge, letters acknowledging his ill-will towards them, asking them for their forgiveness, and proffering his friendship.

The relief which came to him with this decision had a determining effect on his life ; it taught him to believe that there can be no living and transforming sense of unity with the divine Will, no " God Consciousness " as he calls it, so long as the heart is clogged and smothered by any obstinate trace of selfishness. There must be confession, complete and unequivocating restitution.

The fact that he received no replies to his letters did not daunt the happiness which had now come to him from his unbroken sense of the divine companionship. That fact made him realise all the more sharply how hard it is—nay, but impossible—for a proud heart, however virtuous, to enter into the kingdom of love. Moreover, his walk by the lakeside had brought illumination to another man, and now the way was clear before his feet. He had been changed ; he could be the means of changing others.

The logic of this conversion can be expressed in very simple language, and in language which no man of science who has the smallest practical acquaintance with experimental psychology will feel it in his heart to resent.

A will which is divided, which is conscious of opposite tuggings, which is never able to give itself freely either in the one direction or the other, obviously cannot function in the only way proper to a will. It is in a condition fatal to its health, fatal to its nature. Like a muscle seldom exercised, it is on the way to atrophy. One may indeed find it difficult to explain how a will which is not actuated by self-determination—a glad, rejoicing, and never challenged self-determination—can be thought of in any terms of volition, can be named a will.

A man who carries about with him such a will as

this obviously cannot be a happy man. In the sphere of the intellect he may make shift with unsettled opinions, and, like the famous bishop of Browning, exercise his comfortable choice between a life of faith diversified by doubt and a life of doubt diversified by faith. But this will not do in the sphere of action—the true sphere of the will. A man cannot say to himself with any reasonable prospect of happiness, " I will live a life of love diversified by hate," or " I will devote some of my time to seeking truth, and some of it to propagating error." On the face of it, peace of mind demands a coherent will. The will must be doing what it wants to do—be it good or evil—if it is to be unconscious of hindrance.

It is plain to us that the distressed condition of F. B.'s mind was a consequence of his divided will. He half-wanted to do a thing, and he half-wanted not to do that thing. Whether the vision in the little Cumberland church was subjective or objective, whether it was a genuine apparition—that is to say, an operation of spiritual law not yet investigated by the human mind—or a sudden obedience of the physical senses to a morbid pressure of nervous energy, does not seem to me of great importance. The fact which appears salient, and hopeful of intelligent understanding, is the fact that this suffering mind was immediately healed by a decision definitely and absolutely to exercise its will henceforth in one single direction.

There is here no argument for religion. A man half-afraid to go to the devil might find himself delivered from distress of mind by flinging aside his former hesitancies and entering with a whole heart and a whole will into the satanic service. The point is that all success demands the will at the back of it. A man cannot be happy in a life of vice so long as he is conscious of moral scruples ; and a man cannot be happy in a life of virtue so long as any of his inclinations bear him towards vice. The demand of both God and Satan is identical—the whole heart.

The deepest thing in our nature, said William James, is this dumb region of the heart in which we dwell alone with our willingnesses and unwillingnesses; " in these depths of personality the sources of all our outer deeds and decisions take their rise."

This is psychology—the psychology of world history, the psychology of every man's experience. We may hold this same clue in our hands as we go forward to consider the second stage in the conversion of F. B. He found that a great happiness came to him with the decision to exert his unified will in the service of One who proclaimed the reality of the spiritual world, and pronounced the values of instinctive materialism to be illusions. He discovered, in describing this experience to another man, that what had hindered him from long ago making this decision was sin. Sin is a theological term, but it is also a practical term—a term of world history, a term of every man's experience. It signifies error.

Sin is that which hinders the evolution of the human race and the growth of the individual man. It may be drunkenness or a false theory in art. It may be murder or pride ; it may be dishonesty or

Bc

intolerance. It is anything which impoverishes spiritual power, and deflects the personality from fulfilling its highest purposes. Perhaps it is best seen in its effect on a State. Sin brought the glory of Babylonia to the dust. Sin dug the grave of Athens. Sin destroyed so majestic a political experiment as the Roman Empire. Sin—the sin of unconscionable greed wedded to a piety that was either traditional or insincere where it was not actually hypocritical—corrupted the industrial achievements of England in the nineteenth century, and left us a heritage of social problems not yet solved. What sin has done, and is still doing, for Russia, Ireland, Greece, and Turkey, let every man judge for himself.

Another palpable aspect of sin is to be seen in those institutions of civilisation which law and charity erect either for the punishment or the curing of its victims. How many millions of money are spent in every chief country of the world on prisons and police-systems, on lunatic asylums and hospitals, and how many men and women wasted in staffing them? Is not the philanthropy of mankind saddled with huge and increasing liabilities for the children of neglectful and even cruel parents? Are not the navies and armies of Europe, the expense of which presses so heavily on the industrial, political, and domestic life of nations, witnesses to a state of mind wholly at variance with an unbestial outlook? No man will argue either that sin is not responsible for by far the greater part of national expenditure, or that a State would not be in a better position to explore the future of mankind if it were not for its multitudes of sinners.[1] Is it not enough for us that we speak of a particularly contemptible sinner as a " degenerate " ?

In the same fashion, sin operates disastrously in the individual. Its effect is represented by all those motions of his will towards things which offer no ultimate satisfaction to his nature. It stands in his life for hindrance and impediment. It is best described, perhaps, as mutiny towards evolution. The sinner is like a cell in the body which refuses to grow ; it is the cancer of spiritual life. A man cannot do his duty towards the world who is not growing away from that world's past. The immense emphasis laid on sin by religion is justified by the interests of civilisation. The easy forgiveness of sin promised by some of the great Churches of the Christian religion is as perilous to those high interests of civilisation as the thousand enticements of a sensual materialism.

All this, I think, will be accepted by most men. The question remains, How are we to get rid of sin ? How are we to free our wills from the fettering of the past ? It is here that F. B. seems to help us. He says that the degree of our immunity from moral disease is governed absolutely by the degree of our desire for moral health. If we complain that we are slaves to sin, we confess that we desire sin. If we

[1] The cost to Great Britain for the year ending March, 1921, of Law, Justice, Health Insurance, Poor Relief, Reformatories, Child Welfare, Inebriates, and Lunatics exceeded £80,000,000.

say that at certain times we are overtaken by sin, we proclaim that we are not travelling on the road of virtue. Sin is neither footpad nor assassin ; it lives, and can only live, in the heart which does not love goodness with all its strength, with all its earnestness, and with all its appetency.

He came by this conviction in a manner calculated to make an ineffaceable impression on his mind. Soon after his conversion he devoted himself with great enthusiasm to the work of educating in the knowledge of personal religion theological students and other young men following in various ways the religious life. His idea was to help these eager and noble disciples of his Master to be more successful in their sacred work, to teach them how they should lay their main emphasis on personal religion, and how they should guard themselves against the destroying influences of ecclesiastical mechanism. But at the very threshold of this new experience he encountered the old enemy. There, in the heart of even the theological student, he found this old enemy deeply entrenched, sin in one form or another holding the citadel against all the elegant deployments of divinity. In secret the theological student was fighting his sin—perhaps one of those secret sins which prey on spiritual vitality and attack so destructively the sensitive nerve of a man's self-respect ; he was fighting it in various ways, orthodox ways, but fighting it in vain.

Then came enlightenment from F. B. That despised sin could not so tremendously afflict him if he loved goodness. Its strength was not great ; the feebleness of the victim's desire for God alone enabled it to play the part of tyrant; it would disappear as if it had never been immediately he craved for righteousness with his whole heart, his whole spirit. Then followed a new understanding of the great teaching, " *Blessed are the pure in heart, for they shall see God.*"

One of the men who has been constantly in the society of F. B., who has gone with him on missions to many countries in the East as well as to most countries in Europe, spoke to me of the wonderful effect produced by this honest teaching.

" F. B. regards every man with real hope. He often says that a person in pain can easily be healed ; it is the person asleep who tries him hardest. He deals with the secret sinner not emotionally, not credally. He tells him that his sin is ' walling him in from God.' He exposes it as a deliberate structure of the man's will raised against consciousness of God. The man may protest that he desires this consciousness of God, prays for it, hungers for it, that his whole life is directed to acquiring it. F. tells him that he is deceiving himself. He says, ' God comes to us when we ask Him.' If the man again protests that he has asked God again and again to come to him, F. asks, ' With your whole will ? ' Then he explains that the sufferer is attempting to lie to himself, as well as to God, and that it is only disease, this secret sin, which could make him so foolish. From that he proceeds to getting the sin into the open, and showing it to its victim in all its horror and loathsomeness. He uses the knife, for he is a surgeon and no dispenser of

drugs. He doesn't believe in narcotics; he believes
in eradicating the disease, cutting it clean out by the
roots. He is terribly incisive, in love. He makes
you hate your sin, almost yourself, but he makes you
feel he cares for you all the time. After this it is a
matter for the man's will. Hatred of his sin, and a
real longing to be rid of it, a real longing for freedom
and health accompanied by a passionate craving for
the consciousness of God in his soul, sooner or later,
very often immediately, will give him a new will.
It is F.'s ruthless insistence on sin as an act of the
will, a deliberate act, an act of the affections, which
rouses men in this case to confront the truth of their
condition.

" Finally, when he has done his work as a surgeon,
he becomes a physician. He tells men whom he has
thus awakened from sleep or delivered from disease
that they may very easily, all the same, become
spiritually liverish, and spiritually feeble, and spiritually rheumatic, unless they exercise their spiritual
qualities. So he makes them, whatever their professions are or may be, helpers of other men, savers
of other souls. In one way or another they have
to be living unselfishly for the highest sake of other
people. It is in that life, he tells them, they will
find their greatest happiness, because it is only in
such a life that man can enjoy an uninterrupted
consciousness of God."

F. B. says that anything is sin which prevents him
from being a miracle-worker. He teaches that it is
necessary to hate sin, forsake sin, confess sin, and
to make restitution. " This is taking a daily

spiritual bath." The heart must be cleansed of all iniquity.

One whose life has been changed by him, and who is now changing others in a remarkable manner, describes the theory of F. B. in the following way : "There are two seas in Palestine, one in the north teeming with life—fish, fruit, crops, birds, flowers, life of all kinds. In the south is the Dead Sea—no fish, no fruit, no flowers, no houses, no life of any kind. What is the reason for the difference? The Sea of Galilee has a river flowing into it, and a river flowing out of it. The Dead Sea has the same river flowing into it, but none flowing out."

It is a good figure. Science and philosophy will not quarrel with it. A mind which receives and gives is a Sea of Galilee ; a mind which receives, but gives nothing out, is a Dead Sea. It is a law of our nature that we enrich ourselves by sharing with others the accumulations of our activities, be they intellectual or material. The miser of wealth or knowledge punishes no man so heavily as himself.

The reader will perceive, then, that F. B. has common sense and the experience of the human race on the side of his method. He tells men that if they would be happy and undistracted they must be *whole-hearted.* His phrase " God Consciousness " may be translated into " apprehension of the truth," for the highest of which a man is capable is truth. His hours of silence, " listening to God," may be seen as meditation, when the mind listens to the voice of that higher nature which every normal man possesses in himself, and which is the driving force in evolution.   Further, his teaching that we must hate whatever frustrates our growth, and crave with our entire will for those things which increase our powers, is a teaching which needs no religious sanction for the reasonableness of its demands.

Every man, therefore, may make trial of this method, whatever his religious opinions.   Every man who desires to grow, every man who desires peace of heart and strength of mind, may test the truth of this method in his own life, without reference to any religion.   But no man who thus genuinely endeavours to test this teaching will be able to doubt in the end that by discovering and proclaiming this law of man's spiritual nature Jesus, *ipso facto*, revealed himself as the incarnation of universal truth.

As a preface to these narratives I will conclude the present chapter with an explanation of F. B.'s work in the Universities of the world.

Two Anglican bishops in the East, greatly struck by the extraordinary effect of F. B.'s personal revivalism among missionaries, asked him to pay a visit to their sons in Cambridge.   They were anxious that these two boys should know F. B.'s idea of religion on the threshold of their manhood.   That visit revealed to F. B. a very distressing state of things in the colleges of the University.   He called a few of his followers to his side, and began a private work, to all intents and purposes a conversational work, among the undergraduates of Cambridge.

On his return to the United States he set a similar work in motion among the various American

Universities. Then, paying another visit to England, he brought back with him some of the American undergraduates who had become converted ; and, returning once more to America, took with him English undergraduates who had undergone a like experience.

In this work he is engaged at the present moment, and he believes that a new knowledge of religion is spreading among men who may exercise a strong influence on English-speaking civilisation during the next fifty years. Some of these men more or less share his theological opinions ; some are opposed to them ; all, however, are agreed that he has changed their lives, and regard him with an affection which is one of many proofs I possess that his goodness has the true character of divinity—it is lovable.

> Therefore to thee it was given
> Many to save with thyself;
> And at the end of thy day,
> O faithful shepherd! to come,
> Bringing thy sheep in thy hand.

CHAPTER III

GREATS

THE writer of the following narrative is a man twenty-four years of age. He is regarded by many good judges as a scholar who may quite possibly make a valuable contribution to philosophy.

His narrative was written during a busy time in one of the German Universities. It was chiefly intended as a note for my guidance. Its interest, however, seems to me so considerable that I have decided to publish it without interruption. The reader must bear in mind that the writer possesses in a very eminent manner the tentative and balancing mind of a " Greats " man. It will be necessary to make a certain allowance for his antipathetic attitude towards F. B. and also to read between the lines at those crucial moments in the narrative where feeling is vigorously suppressed, and reason, shrinking from a statement of the emotions, escapes from expression in a string of dots. The reader, I hope, will be able to imagine what those dots signify when he knows that this man has suffered very deeply, that through all his sufferings he has kept his courage, and that the most impressive quality of his courage is its unsparing honesty.

Let me say that one of the reasons which induces me to publish the narrative in its original form is the conviction that F. B. will not be able to read so courageous and appealing a statement without seeing that his influence is wholly independent of his theology. If one could set the spirit free from all man-invented forms, how soon might religion arise from its death-bed to save the world from the destructive delusions of materialism.

THE NARRATIVE

This is nothing more than a contribution towards investigating one particular phenomenon—the influence of F. B. And as the most striking feature of his work is that he addresses no monster meetings and writes no books himself, personal reminiscences are the only means available to estimate the aims and value of his work.

It will have been made clear already to the reader that F. B. is at least a remarkable personality, and as such possesses the gift of producing violent reactions in those with whom he comes into contact. There are few men among those who know him at all well who do not feel either an intense liking or an intense dislike for him ; who are not by turns surprised, admiring, disappointed, enthusiastic, disgusted, afraid, or scornful of this apparently commonplace American. This is a very great hindrance to a fair estimate of him. I must, therefore, say at the outset that I write this as far as possible " in a cool hour," after living for nearly six months entirely out of the range of his influence and out of the sound of his name.

Perhaps a personality may be thought of as a

piece of cord tossed from Norn to Norn, as the old
Germans imagined it.   Life at least seems to be an
interplay of elemental forces, which come to the fore
one after another in the time-order, but must work
ever with a material which is never quite formless.

If Wordsworth's conviction—which is also mine—
be correct, then not even the parents of a new-born
child have a perfectly plastic soul before them to
form as they will.

My father was the vicar of a small town in East
Anglia—Cromwell's East Anglia, where the Protestant tradition lies still deep in the heart of the
people.   It was a Protestantism with all the rigidity
of the Scots Protestantism, but without its demo-
cratic sympathies—a Protestantism of the *petit
bourgeois*.   It was impressed upon my youth that
religion was a matter of wearing black clothes,
playing no games, and reading only " Sunday "
books on Sunday ; of reading two " portions " of the
Bible of the appointed length on week-days ; of
attending family prayers, which, one felt instinctively,
was principally for the benefit of the servants, who
sat on three chairs in an exact row in the middle of
the room.   (It was for myself a severe Physical
Exercise, and consisted of kneeling very straight up
in front of a chair which I was not allowed to touch
under pain of continual smacks from my mother.
This was only relieved by the ever-present hope that
something would go wrong, that my father would
read the same prayers twice over or omit some
essential part of the routine, which, indeed, often
occurred, and was the signal for subdued giggling
round the room.)

One can laugh now over much that one then cried about ; but family anecdotes are not here in place ; perhaps Samuel Butler's *The Way of all Flesh* would give the best impression of the religious environment of my boyhood. And this religion did play a very considerable part in my life, and I took it as much a matter of course as being washed and dressed. I can only state as a fact that when I was first sent to school at the age of eight I knew an immense quantity of the Bible by heart, a knowledge which was useful in gaining me all the Divinity Prizes for which I ever competed. I had no inkling that my environment was in any way peculiar before I went to school ; I had scarcely any playmate except my younger sister, and, later, my brother. Did I reflect upon it at all ? It is hard to say.

I will relate only two incidents, one told against me by my mother, the other which I remember very keenly as happening not later than my fifth year. My mother tells how, when three years old, after much admonition for some naughtiness or other I replied, " Though dark my path and sad my lot, I will be still and murmur not." She adds that she has no idea where I could have heard the words. The other is the emotional recollection associated with a punishment by a particular nurserymaid. I had had read to me the Sermon on the Mount. I had a particular affection for bacon fat, which was always a subject of dispute between my sister and me at breakfast. *Ergo*, thought I, I must give up my portion of bacon fat to her next day. The nurserymaid was unsympathetic, and my venture in unselfishness was treated as defiance of the powers

that be. On the ground of other specific recollec-
tions I can say certainly that I was perplexed, first,
how to square the treatment of the servants with my
knowledge of the Bible—I think I always felt a
certain sympathy with them, as also in the power of
these other two beings who were on such intimate
terms with God that they alone knew what He would
punish and what He would reward—and, second, as
to the wickedness of mentioning sexual matters.
Until I went to school I was subject to no strong
influence other than that of my parents (whom up
to this date I hardly differentiated) and my uncles
and aunts, of whom later.

My impression is that in the first stage " God "
meant to me absolutely nothing but the power of my
parents. I think it would not otherwise have been so
easy to obliterate him on first going to school. I at
once lost my sense of obligation to perform those
prayers and Bible readings, and very soon I gave up
the performance of them too. I do not connect the
school chapel services with the slightest degree of
religious sentiment. I had violent fluctuations of
happiness and unhappiness, but did not connect
them with religion in any way. When, at the age
of ten, a serious-minded tutor tried to convert me,
I laughed him into giving up the attempt. All that
was silly ; a sign of weakness. My ideal at that
time, I remember, was the " wily Odysseus " ; I
made up my mind to accomplish in the school
through diplomacy what seemed through lack of
athletic prowess impossible. To some extent I
succeeded. I thought : " One day I shall be able
to manage my father too."

In this temper of cynical Positivism I was probably a very unamiable person when, at thirteen, I left my private school for one of the big public schools. I was deservedly, if somewhat severely, repressed in my first two years there, and distaste for my home grew with my unhappiness at school. I could no longer play with my sister, and I had found no other interests there. I was rather forcibly driven in upon myself. My antipathy to my parents grew and grew during these two years, till it assumed the proportions of a black cloud over my life, and was invested with the characteristics of all the tyrants and monsters who were ready to hand in the history lessons, and particularly in the Greek history. I remember a letter to my father at about my fourteenth year in which I held ardently in the spirit of Herodotus or Sophocles on the necessity of obeying my tutor as officer of the school to which I belonged, and the necessity of disobeying him as mere instrument of autocratic parents. I attributed every misfortune which befell me at school to the secret machinations of my parents with the authorities. The God of my childhood had gradually become my Devil.

At this stage the conflict had certainly no strictly religious significance. From the religious point of view, perhaps, the only event of note was the growing influence in my fourteenth and fifteenth years of a somewhat older boy, who introduced me to the mysteries of Anglo-Catholicism. He was a personality likely to attract ; diversely brilliant, subtle, humorous, combining with these intellectual gifts a sympathy which later degenerated into softness. His influence was very transitory, but I learned from him two things which were not so unconnected as they appear. First he really re-awoke my belief in the possibility of a real personal religion, which, in spite of its elaborate appeal to my intellectual snobbishness, was far more real and vital than anything I had experienced before. From that moment religion became a factor in my life, curious as were the phases that it underwent. Second, he taught me to admire Swinburne.

Curiously enough, I soon after came up against real religion in the other camp, through a visit to an extremely pious Protestant lady who tried to persuade me, by means of the book of Revelation and an equation of the Beast with the Roman Catholic Church, that the world would come to an end in 1915. I was really upset by this point of view, and prayed continually for a miracle to decide which of the two extremes was favoured by God. But this Protestantism had no chance, with its superficial relationship to the religion of my home. I stealthily read Catholic books, and gloried in the possession of a God in whom my parents had no part nor lot. I was immensely happier now. Under the spell of it I was confirmed.

This development lasted, if I remember rightly, about eighteen months. Together with concurrent " good fortune " (?) of various sorts it had an effect on my life. I found in the Communion Service more than I had believed possible. In the end it broke inevitably on the one hidden rock of insincerity. I had the first open outburst of violence against my parents shortly before my confirmation, in which I let off the suppressed emotions of years. I was repressed after that more than ever, and humiliated before my greatest friends ; in return I comforted myself with the Imprecatory Psalms.

About eighteen months after my confirmation matters came to a crisis in this direction. From seventeen till twenty-two I was occupied above all things in a long and bitter struggle against my parents. . . . Starting with a quarrel about money, it involved eventually my sister and brother, most of my relatives, and most of my teachers. There were periods of superficial calm, but I think the feeling of tension and the desire to avoid each other was at no time absent during that period, and the fact of the struggle had a very great effect on my internal development.

I feel still that there was something elemental and necessary about the struggle. It was a fight for a bare minimum of freedom, which had to come sooner or later, but it was embittered by the religious problems involved. It was easy enough to form the idea that my father was acting dishonestly ; easy also to believe that he was ill-treating my sister and trying to separate her from me. To all such reproaches my father had one method of reply—a deluge of lectures, sermons, pamphlets, threatening the wrath of God upon anyone who ventured to question anything that their parents said or did. This was accompanied by more practical threats through the medium of my house master, and eventually the head master. I got from them much real but timid sympathy, as I thought it ; I got from another official of the school not only the degree of independence which I needed to avoid my home in the holidays, and to avoid having to ask for pocket money, but also a lasting friendship which had a great effect upon my life.

But at first I had no such older friend to lean upon. I played eagerly my father's own game ; I countered his texts with other texts ; I felt a certain *Schadenfreude* in this diplomatic game of trying to put the other party in the wrong.   Only it was no game then, but terrible earnest ; I felt myself a Crusader, not only for my freedom, but for my God, for the protection of the Oppressed (my younger brother and sisters), for Liberty of Belief.   Perhaps I lived again the history of my people of East Anglia.   I did believe passionately in a God who was compatible with reason and liberty of thought, and when I expressed these sentiments, I was told that I must be kept from contaminating my family with such dangerous ideas.   I was denounced on all occasions as an Atheist and Socialist.   I had then no notion of the economic significance of Socialism ; I was under the influence of Bernard Shaw and William Morris, but still more of Tolstoy.   As a prefect and as a cadet officer I tried to put my Tolstoyian principles into effect, with rather mixed success.   As is usual with youth, I painted everything in vivid whites and blacks.   As secretary of a debating club I undertook a campaign against corrupt elections.   I refused to make use of my privilege of " fagging " the smaller boys.   I practised asceticisms, such as having no fire in my room for a whole winter, or sitting up and meditating all night.   But perhaps that belongs to a later stage.

I said to myself one day, " What if I *am* an

Atheist? What if my father represents, not a misstatement of Christianity, but Christianity in itself and in its essence? All the tyrants and obscurantists since the world began have based their claims on Divine Right, on a Divine Revelation where there is no room for reason. All the religious wars which have devastated the earth have sprung from this essence of Christianity as a Revealed Religion. It can have no place in a world of democracy and enlightenment."

My hero was no longer Tolstoy; Shelley and Swinburne inspired my hopeful moods, and Marcus Aurelius and the Buddha my depressions. The last I owed to a very gifted boy whom I knew at that time, for me one of the great losses of the war. I threw myself into my new mission, which was nothing less than the destruction of Christianity.

I called myself a Pantheist, and the sense of the unseen remained strong with me. But I never missed an opportunity of diverting an essay or a speech into a polemic against Christianity. I devoted much ingenuity to making out St. Paul to be a Pantheist; I spent hours of argument upon the head master; with the greatest difficulty I obtained permission to recite Swinburne's " Hymn to Man " to the assembled school; and finally I deluged my father with blasphemies, spoken, written, and printed. Perhaps this was the motive of the whole; I think it does not explain everything.

Out of the many personalities who left their mark upon my school life, of whom I make no mention, I must except the new head master, who came on the scene during my last terms. He was a man whom I admired at once for his intellect, and came gradually to love for the greatness of soul concealed under a somewhat capricious humour. He was the first person who was neither shocked nor contemptuous over my anti-Christian crusade ; he made me feel that he was personally sorry, and that I was missing the greatest thing in the world. He infected me with his own enthusiasm for his own heroes, St. Paul, St. Francis, Amos, Browning. He was a hero-worshipper. He also had in a very high degree the sense of God in nature and in history which had always been with me to some extent, only, on account of his personal Christianity, it was in him a living, moving force. He gave me the impulse to worship ; he convinced me that for a keen and candid mind Christianity was compatible with liberty. He is not understood, perhaps through his own fault. He did not make Christianity practical in my life, but he was a very great inspiration for the coming years.

My years in the army, from the religious point of view, were blank and meagre. My longed-for financial independence improved my relationship with my parents for a few months, until a much more serious cause of trouble arose. I conceived that they were trying by baseless slanders to cut me off from all my friends and to bring me into trouble with my regimental authorities. I did what I knew would most hurt my mother's affection and my father's pride ; I refused to see them before being sent to France.

The reply was a storm of denunciatory tracts, which followed me everywhere around France and Germany,

letters rejoicing at the judgment of God when I
failed in an examination, letters announcing my
father's determination to prevent me getting a job
or going to the University until I proved more
tractable and apologised for my conduct. The
atmosphere of a fashionable regiment was not favour-
able. I hardened and embittered my heart, and set
myself to win a materially full life, if the stars in
their courses fought against me.

In this spirit I went to Oxford, almost without
money or hope of having enough to live upon. And
yet my belief in God was never quite dead. Three
things kept it alive—a change of station to the
Yorkshire moors, my first taste of the hills, with all
that that means ; a couple of months lived among
some very unfortunate people, which made me
conscious of my longing and of my ineffectiveness to
help ; and, most of all, an act of absolutely unexpected Christian generosity, which enabled me to live
at Oxford and re-awoke my sense of the undeserved
goodness of God to me. For the second time in my
life He saved me through the intervention of an
absolute stranger from a belief that selfish materialism is the only active force among mankind.

My University years were years of rebuilding. The
systematic study of philosophy and of remote
history, into which I plunged passionately, had an
overwhelming effect. It took the edge off my harsh
dogmatisms. I attacked Christianity, as before, at
every opportunity in debate and private argument,
but in a different spirit. I began to wish it might be
true. I preached Socialism as the truth of Christianity. I could not help being impressed by the

college chaplain and by the " Religion and Life " group in Oxford, who seemed to have a real religion which was compatible with freedom and honesty of thought. But above all I was impressed by two undergraduate friends, temperamentally very different from each other and from myself, in no way remarkable in the college except as being real Christians.

One of them, M., was a man considerably older than myself, who, after a career in the Civil Service, had decided to give up his prospects there and become ordained in the English Church. He had no particular intellect, and I own with shame to having felt sometimes embarrassed by his company, but he had a great heart. He used to treat me like a father, sharing all my depressions and irritations. He used to flatter my vanity by asking my opinion " as a philosopher " upon theological questions ; and when I railed against the Church he would answer me as far as he could, and when he could not, then he would beam all over and say softly to himself, " Dear creature ! " I came to know gradually of his influence in other quarters of the college ; he felt a mission to " heal those who are broken in heart." He had a mystical and contemplative temperament, which was quite compatible with a taste for giving riotous dinner-parties.

My other friend, J., was peculiarly unlike him in most respects. A person of abundant energy, he used to butt about the world, breaking his head against all the walls of unreason and unrighteousness he could find. He was absolutely fearless, and participated in every mad rag which undergraduate ingenuity could devise. He used to campaign furiously against every abuse in the college and in favour of all the " depressed classes " of the University—the workmen of Ruskin College, the scouts, the women, and the Indians. He had little theoretical but much practical interest in discussion ; he had a pathetic belief in the possibility of convincing people by reason, and used to spend his time bringing incompatible people together at meals for their mutual education. He had a great gift of winning the confidence of absolute strangers, such as Japs and peasant women. He was absolutely irrepressible and indepressible.

I had the privilege of travelling with him a good deal in the country. I learned there what the keeping in touch with God through prayer meant to him. I envied him his strength and I envied his absolute thoughtlessness for himself. Many were our discussions, lasting far into the night, round a fire, curled up in the arm-chairs which only Oxford understands, or lying in a canoe under the moonlight and the willows of the Hinksey stream.

We would talk with that sense of leisure and delight in pure argument for its own sake that one only has during one's first year at the University, when one has not yet learned to shrink before the great unsolved questions of the world. We were both reading philosophy. I was thoroughly under the spell of Hegel (not the subjective nihilists who claim to be his followers in England, but the master himself) and of Plato, whom I rediscovered through the great German idealists. I think I clung to this belief in the progress of Reason through the world, not because I could see her traces, but just because I could not see them. Where others went easily by instinct, I felt I had to beat out a way painfully through the jungle of things. My earth was so formless and void it must conceal somewhere the form-giving Spirit. Life could not be just this that I experienced. I could not rid myself of the persuasion that St. Paul formulated, but which is the essence of the teaching of all the great philosophers in Greece and in Germany: " We *know* that all things work together for good." " The world-history is the purpose of God, which all in all is being fulfilled."

I had also a kind of mystical belief that the great saints and prophets on the earth had understood this purposiveness of the world's history and been satisfied. I thought with Augustine of " that moment of Understanding which we longed for, which were the fulfilment of that promise, ' Enter thou into the joy of thy Lord.' " I had a curious experience about a year before meeting F. B. My friend M., mentioned above, tried to persuade me to come over with him one day to the theological college in the country where he intended to go on leaving Oxford. I said it would amuse me to see this new sort of Zoo, where all the prospective clerics were gathered together; I never missed a chance of jeering at M.'s future profession. The impression I got from my visit was not at all what I expected. I could not evade the feeling that these otherwise commonplace people had a secret resource somewhere, a certain security about their life which it was a joy to feel. I attributed the feeling rather unsuccessfully to the beauty of the place and the easy simplicity of their life; I knew that I had felt the breath of the Spirit of God. And I said, " How is it that the Christians have preserved something divine and living, in spite of their allegiance to a dead revelation and an obscurantist organisation—in spite of their immoral belief that a forgiveness of sins and benefits after death can be obtained through the recitation of some ill-understood formulæ—in spite of their barbarous myth that God, to appease His own anger, demanded the sacrifice of an innocent person ? " And I set to work furiously on comparative religion and mythology, on Frazer, and Reinach, and Rohde, to prove to others and satisfy myself that all these Christian dogmas and rituals were old before Jesus appeared on the stage ; that other religions had produced as high a morality and as high a culture ; that the Christians could not claim a monopoly of the Divine Spirit, which had spoken from the poets and prophets and philosophers of every age.

One Saturday night I was writing an essay upon the idea of the soul, which I had been trying to trace through the early stages of European culture, when J. burst into my room, very excited. " Hello," he cried. " I've got a brand new phenomenon for you." He proceeded to tell me about F. B.

" But what does he do ? " I asked.

" Oh, he just goes around waking up the individual."

" Well, I don't want to see him then ; I don't want to be vaguely enthused ; there's too much of that about the world already."

" But he's a regular prophet ; he believes actively in the Spirit."

" Well, I don't believe he is a Christian then,"
I said ; " the Christians have long put the Spirit
away on the shelf ; they bring Him out once a
year on Whit-Sunday, and then forget about Him
again."

He looked at his watch. " Well, this is Whit-
Sunday," he said. . . .

Later in the day I made my first acquaintance
with F. B. I had severe toothache at the time, and
was having a nerve slowly killed, and was feeling very
disagreeable. I asked him about his travels. He
told me some of his " yarns." The general theme
was that " crows are black the whole world
over."

" But I don't feel conscious of any particular
sin," I said. " I have heard this stuff from my youth,
and it all seems so irrelevant. I wish I were capable
of committing some really great sin. It's just lack
of opportunity, or, still more, lack of imagination.
Your ' interesting sinners ' had to be *born* interesting.
I dream and criticise and never get anywhere definite.
If only one knew what one had to do. . . ." And
perhaps my attention turned upon my own inner
soreness, and I forgot that two minutes ago I had
been trying to decide how to get rid of the man. I
forgot the unpleasantness of his voice ; in fact, he
hardly seemed to be there ; he seemed to feel my
dissatisfaction with things too well ; he was no
longer a second focus of consciousness, but was
somehow sharing in mine.

" You are disorganised," he said, " without a
centre—without Christ."

Another man came in on a casual errand. It was

like the switching on of the lights in a cinema. One's
mind is not adapted for working on two levels at
once. The silent figure in the corner had somehow
set it going on the lowest level ; the superficial
didn't come easily. My visitor saw, I think, my
embarrassment, and soon left.

F. B. began to ask me about my life. I felt somehow that I was on my trial, though not that this
American was in any way concerned in it. I
answered coolly and clearly.

" Well, I'm pleased to have met you, Mr. ——,"
he said, getting up. . . .

Something overwhelming came over me. It was
an insult to play with this man. . . .

. . . "And I also *lie*," I continued in my narrative.
" That is, usually. For instance, what I told you
five minutes ago . . . "

I felt somewhat paralysed, as do probably all
irresolute people after having let loose the irrevoc-
able, but profoundly happy.

" God told me," he said.

He told me about his listening to God and of the
Bible as the mouthpiece of the living Spirit ; of the
guidance of Jesus Christ here and now in the everyday decisions of life. A riot of new possibilities
began to break into the dimness of my mental outlook. I prayed rather definitely.

I walked to the gate with him ; I was feeling
elated as never before. " I seem to have lost control
of myself to-night," I said ; "how absurd all this will
seem to-morrow ! "

" You've heard about the seven devils," he said.
" Get going at once."

I walked by the river with another in the early morning, and it was as when the morning stars sang together, but after breakfast the whole events of the night before seemed hardly credible. " He is a psycho-analyst," I said, " although I didn't notice any of their tricks. We'll see if his stunt with the Bible works."

I hunted out a Bible and turned up by chance the story of the paralytic man. " What does all the business about the forgiveness of sins mean? Which *is* easier to say . . . ? ' But that ye may know that the Son of Man hath power to forgive sins.' . . . What about my toothache last night ? "

I have dwelt on this first meeting rather because of its immediate strangeness than because of its results. For the first time in my life I had deliberately and gladly made a fool of myself before a perfect stranger. I had told him things I had never breathed to another ; I had told him of all my laughable vanities and dishonesties that make the stuff of a man's most intimate life. I put it all down to some uncanny personal quality of the man, some quasi-hypnotic influence. (I believe now that religion has nothing to fear in psychological explanations of the working of God, though these do not carry one very far.) I can only say that I was fairly on my guard against such influences, after what I had heard from J. ; and I must emphatically deny, in view of what is said in some quarters against F. B., that I was in any particular trouble at the time.

" Psychological or not, is this experience the voice of God ? " That was for me the question. I answered, hesitantly but decidedly, " No ! " Any

half-savage thaumaturge playing skilfully on the
chords of the mind could awaken such a momentary
emotion. And my prejudice against Christianity
in general, and against the religion of the Protestant
sects in particular, rose up like a mist.

I saw F. B. no more, but had an invitation from
him some days afterwards to attend his " house-
party " at Cambridge on August 6th. I was pleased
to have a really good excuse for not going—two
successive invitations in the South of England which
would make a return to Cambridge impossible. But
about August 3rd I received three letters, two saying
that owing to unexpected illness my invitations had
fallen through, one from F. B. saying that he was
expecting me at Cambridge. I was very annoyed
with the presumption of the man ; I wrote and told
him so. But my curiosity was too strong ; I
went.

I will confine myself to the subjective impressions I
received at that " house-party." First, one must
take into account the natural attractiveness of even
a Cambridge college in the summer. Second, I was
surprised by the personnel. They were a very mixed
lot, with perhaps a preponderance of the " Rugger
Blue " type of undergraduate, but they were very
natural, and seemed to have left the clique spirit
behind. There were there three other Americans
apart from F. B., and they mixed up with the rest
very creditably. The soul of the party, F. B.
himself, was very unobtrusive. He refused to
preside at any of the meetings, but one knew without
looking for him whether he was there or not. One
admired his seeming carelessness about the success of

his show. It was a bold idea bringing two distinguished speakers on the first night, but it broke down our first shyness. One felt already that the " walls were shaking."

Only all that that phrase implies was at that time new to me. There was hardly a trace of the hard religious dogmatism which I had gone there to find ; but in so far as there was, I could not feel it. I was absorbed in a new experience. I felt as if I was living upon a mountain-top right up against the sky, with the other peaks near and naked against the sun— peaks which it would take hours to reach along the devious, man-made tracks across the valley. And there was nothing left but the claims of God and of the other man standing there before God. And I saw that it was the sins of our choosing, the fear and shame, with which we tie ourselves about, which prevent us from living always thus simply and nobly. I saw also that it was all these things which debar us from a living *faith* in God ; that one can only trust a person from whom one has nothing to conceal ; that only this faith in the tireless working of God in our lives could let loose our buried energies, could bring us to take risks with our wealth and reputation. " Sin blinds, sin binds " ; it could hardly be put better than in this catchword of F. B.'s—Christianity not as imprisonment, but as a Liberation of the soul !

This is all too vague and subjective, and yet I must emphasise one point. I do not remember the substance of F. B.'s speeches ; it was not that which counted. I could and did in the group-discussion argue quite coldly against some of the points which he or his supporters seemed to over-emphasise. It was a particular individual experience which I have had but few times in my life, and perhaps never with the same intensity—the experience I have described above as " standing before God." Whatever I may subsequently think of F. B. cannot alter my conviction on this subject.

I walked up and down the Quad much of one night, pleading against the hardness of the tasks that were set me to do. I had to tackle my parents ; I had to tackle a man I had known and feared at school, the last person in the world I would have chosen to talk to upon this sort of subject ; I had to put myself to shame before certain members of the party. I had, beside the practical questions, the whole theory of this new *Weltanschauung* to tackle. And I said, " This time I am sure it is God's doing, and that He won't let me down."

It was nearly a year before I saw F. B. again, a year of hopes and disappointments. I had immediately to face my home and family ; I had to face some earnest Cambridge undergraduates who were conducting a missionary campaign in my little town, and who nearly drove me into the wilds of revolt again. I have found it hard to believe that the denunciation of one's fellow-Christians is not of the essence of Christianity ; so much energy and enthusiasm are spent upon it. It is hard for us human beings, to whom accidents of personality count so much, to remember that it is neither Paul nor Apollos that matters, " but God that giveth the increase." I heard many months afterwards that even this personal clash brought its harvest. Perhaps it is only through such clashes that we learn slowly and painfully to separate the essence of the teaching of Christ from the purely individual elements in the personality of the teacher. Personality, the medium of all religion, is by no means an unequivocal conception. It is a recurrent charge against F. B. that " his disciples " are excessively dependent on him, take their experience from him at second hand. In most respects, however, we can only picture our relation to Christ through the personal relationships that we have experienced ourselves. Such experience should warn us not to expect to go too fast. When anyone has lived many years in mutual distrust of his fellows it is the work of a few hours— maybe a single act of faith, of willingness to humiliate himself—and the other comes out to meet him, comes further than he had dreamed ; but it is the work of months, maybe of years, in spite of the best will in the world on both sides, to wipe away all the effects. There is much to unlearn.

Those of us who were at Cambridge, and had felt there something new come into our lives, formed a little circle at Oxford with the object of keeping that spirit alive by maintaining touch with each other. Perhaps we were all somewhat discouraged by the meagreness of immediate result. We had to contend with the damp warmth of the Oxford atmosphere, spiritual as well as physical, which is the enemy of heroic resolutions. I had to contend with the comparatively hard and monotonous work of the last year before " schools " (the final examination), and with the excuse it afforded for " minding one's own business " unduly. I had shrunk before the thought

of this year before " schools," with all my friends
" gone down " ; it was better than I could have
imagined. This faith which I had caught a glimpse
of opened both my eyes and my mouth. I began to
learn that I was not the only unfortunate in the
world. I slowly began to think of doing something
for the people with whom I was brought in contact,
instead of thinking only of getting something out
of them. By looking on them as opportunities, in
this way I began gradually to lose my fear of
strangers, a fear which I had come to regard as
inevitable. But also I discovered things that had
been happening around me for two years without my
having any notion of their existence. I began to see
a little of the picture that St. Paul describes as the
" whole creation travailing in pain," and to feel my
helplessness before this fundamental fact of the
world. The many people whom I came across " by
chance," by following the indications of God's guidance, which were sometimes unquestionable, people
who were for one reason or another almost losing
hope, to whom I had to try to impart something of
the faith I had caught sight of—this was sometimes
the only thing in the world that kept up my own
faith. This may read like Pragmatism ; it appeared
to me rather as the continual confirmation of a belief
which I would gladly have disbelieved. I felt myself
again and again before the question, " Am I willing
to make a fool of myself for the sake of another ? "
Or, rather, I felt it not as a question, but as an order,
in circumstances where I could see no reason for it ;
on the occasions when I obeyed it, timidly and half-
heartedly, I never found the command unnecessary.

Cc

Also during this time I began to beat out a working theory to fit my experience. This came about probably through an old acquaintance but new friend among the undergraduates of my college. I had long admired his knowledge, but looked down upon his rather naïve enthusiasms. I had thought him rather " bourgeois "—a snobbish term for something that is peculiarly uncongenial to the bulk of those who have suffered from a public school education. I discovered gradually the goodness of his heart. I do not mean in this connection that I took over his theories. He belonged to the respectable High Church of the seventeenth century and the older Tractarians ; but he believed sincerely and actively in his Church, and was at all times ready to defend it. He had an immense and varied acquaintance, who laughed at him and loved him. In the course of discussion with him my ideas began to shape themselves. He formed one of a small group who met to discuss the Philosophy of Religion. Its regular membership consisted of a Roman Catholic, a Jew, a young Modernist theologian, two mild Agnostics, a very naïve American Atheist, and a pious, rather narrow Nonconformist. But the lines were already laid for me. On my return from Cambridge in the summer my father asked me to read and criticise one of the book of essays which are the product of the very remarkable group of liberal Christians in Oxford who are associated with the name of Canon Streeter. I did find in the works of this group a theory of Christianity which was compatible with freedom and progress of thought, and with the demands of practical experience.

From the theoretical standpoint I had always had two fundamental convictions upon the nature of the world. I was on the one hand attracted by the newer Evolutionism of Bergson and his disciples. From this source, but perhaps more from my anthropological reading, I thought of the world as an endless flux, in which no beliefs, scientific, moral, or religious, could survive more than a few hundred years. Such a view has a special attraction for our generation, the generation which has grown up in the war period and seen " the old faiths ruin and rend." Positivism has never had such a slump in the intellectual world as at the present time. At the same time I could not help believing that this development had a Meaning, a Value, which was somehow related to our values ; I could not banish from my mind the great assertion of the Idealistic tradition that " all we have thought or hoped or dreamed of good shall exist . . . when eternity reaffirms the conception of an hour." But how to imagine the conjuncture of these two postulates of experience, how to picture a world in which all our beliefs are transitory and in which we yet can *know* that all our beliefs are transitory !

The notion of a self-revealing God, a God who, out of blindly reacting animals, is creating Personal Souls in his own image ; of this world of pleasure and sin as an Education, in the sense of Stevenson's prayer ; of the revelation of this " mystery " through the incarnation of Christ, the " Logos "—all this was new and wonderful to me, and supplied a theoretical want no less than a practical. My mind leaped back to the later Epistles of St. Paul, where he develops this idea of " God in Christ reconciling the world to Himself," of Christ as the head of a body of creatures grown conscious of their Creator. This again connected itself with a host of mystical speculations which are the common property of our age—an age awaking to the importance of the Unconscious and to the multiplicities of Personality. I have found them recently set forth by a German novelist, Gustav Meyrin, in his book *The White Dominican*. I only wish to emphasise the fact that from the orthodox Christian point of view my theory was at that time, to say the least of it, deficient. The view of the Atonement to an angry God through a vicarious sacrifice, the view that treats the words of Christ as a Law and God as a policeman, was abhorrent to me. I was also not prepared to admit that the sin of individuals could disorder the plan of the universe. I felt that this latter was in conflict with all the postulates of theoretical activity, just as the former doctrines struck at the root of all practical activity. In regard to the reality of sin, I would only go as far as Cleanthes' prayer: " O God, let me follow out Thy will gladly ; for if through evil desire I struggle against it to my own sorrow, yet must I follow it none the less." Sin harms the individual soul of the sinner ; it cannot harm God, nor, if this seem paradox, can it harm other souls. Perhaps it was the inherited Calvinism of my fathers coming to the surface. Calvinism can be a very unattractive doctrine, but the notion of the overruling power of God to which it holds fast is of the essence of all religion whatever. It was the overwhelming belief in the power of God here and now that inflamed the saints and prophets and heroes from the beginning of time. Was it possible to have a faith which could be progressive and liberal, and yet possess the power to move mountains? I believed then that it was. Perhaps the existence of such a prophet in a prominent position in Oxford was the only ground I had then for such a belief. My greatest debt during this time is owed to Dr. Selbie, although he was then unknown to me personally. His was the voice of one who, like Plato's philosopher-king, had climbed to the heights, without losing his bearings when he returned to the valleys. He was so unlike F. B. in every way, and like him in one respect—his religion was *alive*.

Thus, though not unconscious of my theoretical differences from F. B., it was this unmistakable living quality in his religion that made me await his return with eager expectation. Here was a man who could stir even Oxford. He did. How, I am at a loss to explain. He sat for two weeks in a room in one of the colleges, and by the end of his stay the college was ranged sharply apart in two camps—the pro- and anti-F. B.'s. He addressed a meeting in the college soon after his arrival, at which an influential section of the undergraduates came with a concerted scheme to " rag " this impudent American. And somehow they felt their witticisms out of place, and the attack fell rather flat. Perhaps it was just the quiet confidence of the man that his enemies could not help feeling. Or one may repeat a second-hand story of how he led a petulant committee up to the top of Shotover Hill and harangued them upon their sins, with the effect that they one and all tried to resign. His whole stay in Oxford was an incredible *tour de force*. Was it more than that ?

That, in the nature of the case, can never be answered by a human observer. 1 believe he brought help and " Good News " to many. I think I was somewhat disappointed with the immediate results in the " test-cases " I had mentally set him. You cannot write answers on a human personality as on a piece of foolscap. And I found it a little hard to answer the charge that much of his following was obtained by the questionable method of making lurid confessions of sins in meetings. " Can this gospel be of God, if it be spread by playing upon the fears of the nervous and inexperienced ? " This was the question that many people whom I respected put to me at that time. I had doubts like the rest, but I had opportunities of knowing him more intimately than the rest. My mockery faded away into self-reproach at the first contact with his simple goodness. My natural embarrassment at being mixed up with this crank preacher at all was a spur to me to defend him more vigorously. I attributed all my doubts to the misrepresentations of his disciples.

His disciples ? Perhaps therein lay the false conception that was the cause of my difficulties. It is easy to feel the emotion behind the great hymn of St. Francis, difficult to live it out in everyday life : " Let the Lord God be praised in *all* His creatures."

Is it possible in the last resort to distinguish Christianity from the opinions and prejudices of all other Christians whatever, without one's own belief becoming thereby thin and ineffective ? My belief in Christ began to detach itself gradually from my belief in F. B. A few days' stay with my friend in his theological college mentioned above brought to my consciousness the fact that this Christianity had gnawed its way into my life. One morning in a wood on top of the Chilterns I felt irresistibly that Christ was calling me to some definite work. What it might be I had no idea. I was afraid before this " amaranthine weed." Also I knew the vagueness and ineffectiveness of my temperament, to which F. B. was like a cold bath. With all this in mind, I accepted an offer of his to travel round Europe with him in the summer as tutor to a friend of his. I said I should go unreservedly under his orders, under a vow of " holy obedience." It should be the discipline that was the essence of " Continuance."

The second house-party was a foretaste of the continental pilgrimage ; indeed, I met there most of the personnel of the " F. B. troupe "—as an observer once called it—for the first time. The atmosphere was not at all like that of the Cambridge party of the year before ; the element of the Professional Christian who has a pet doctrine to expound was much more in evidence. The first two days were peculiarly inharmonious ; criticism was in the air. I found much that was uncongenial to me in the views and manners of the " disciples," but at the same time I discovered ever new qualities to admire in the " master." He had hardly spoken in the first two days, but he knew what we were saying, and was quite unperturbed by it. " Wait," I said to his detractors, " wait till he really takes things in hand."

The end of the house-party was the greatest personal triumph for F. B. that could have been imagined. The lion lay down with the lamb. It will have been adequately described elsewhere in this book. I went away, after lunching with a man I had once described as " the most unsympathetic I could imagine," with the voice that Peter heard sounding in my ears : " What God hath cleansed, that call not thou common."

The " continental tour," which gave me the most adequate insight into the personality and work of F. B., is difficult for me to describe in any detail, because it involved rather intimately the affairs of others, which I do not feel justified in bringing into print. It was a very severe lesson in practical internationalism. The " troupe " were all Americans [1] —which, however, should not be taken as a sufficient description of them. We had one other Englishman with us, a former acquaintance of mine, who joined the party as it was leaving England under somewhat peculiar circumstances. He was always there under protest, had considerable powers of observation, and used to turn the tap of his rather venomous humour continuously upon the Americans and their friends. I was always told off to look after him, and he was a great strain upon my loyalty to F. B. I was in a sense the cause of his joining the party. I had introduced him to F. B. because I believed he was in need of something that F. B. could give him. I cannot leave D. altogether out of the story, because he was in some sense one side of myself—the side that rebelled against the particular religious forms of the Americans. To explain what I mean I must introduce

[1] The host, I understand, was a very original and hearty Canadian, who not only paid the piper but set the tune.—H. B.

an idea which was very well expressed to me by a German friend : " You English," he said, " are always at the mercy of your ' Æsthetic Conscience.' You have an instinctive reaction against some forms of behaviour which seem out of place, vulgar, theatrical. This Æsthetic Conscience is right ninety-nine times out of a hundred ; in the hundredth case it will prevent you from helping or appreciating a man whose constitution or education are radically different from your own." My Æsthetic Conscience had a hard time of it with the Americans. My tutorial work never materialised. If it had not been for D.—my departure would have left him in a peculiarly awkward position—I should have packed up and left the party. I felt myself in an alien culture, and it was quite clear that the other members of the party felt the same of me. I hardly saw F. B. ; plans were made and changed over my head ; I was physically tired with the perpetual travelling, and felt utterly in the dark. For the sake of D. I had to keep up my spirits and the honour of F. B. I spoke of the Diversity of Manners and the Identity of Principles. I was aware of the great complex of prejudices which I have called the " Æsthetic Con-science "—all too aware of it. I had lost confidence in my own values. I found myself in a state of utter bewilderment at the utter relativity of things. I said one day gravely enough to a German friend, who in a fit of absence of mind had poured sugar instead of salt on his egg : " I see it is the custom of your country to eat sugar with your eggs." That was what I felt like with the Americans. A severe disappointment over " schools " a couple of weeks before had completed my discouragement. I felt I *was* inefficient according to the American hustling standards, and the knowledge made me more inefficient than ever. F. B. never missed an opportunity of pointing out the fact to me. I told him once that living with him involved running one's head up against a stone wall whenever one tried to exercise any initiative of one's own ; the only possible course was to follow orders passively. He used to lecture me with perfect justice on my " obtuseness " ; he did really increase my powers of observation. He was too infallible ; I wondered at the cleverness and the energy of the man ; I began to feel more and more alienated from him.

And then a wonderful day came. We had just arrived in Brussels. The journeys always made me feel irritable. I had made up my mind to go at any price. Things were simplified for me. D. was so unusually rude to F. B. that it was decided that he would have to leave the party. I was "detailed" to take him on with me to my destination in Germany. I had a weary day trying to make plans for D. I came to see F. B. in the evening to make final arrangements. He was in bed. I thanked him formally for all he had done and told him what I meant to do. . . . And he looked at me very much moved, and said : " Clive, I have one thing to say to you before you go. I have got to ask your pardon. I've left you in the dark and in the cold. I'm sorry." . . . I was overwhelmed ; this from my superman ? Anything but this. And he began to pour out all his hopes and anxieties, his plans and his disappointments. " No, no," I said, " you don't know, you

don't know how I have suspected you and slandered
you. . . . If I had only known . . . " My stone wall
had become suddenly human. *Become ?* My mind
went racing backwards over our travels, and I saw
that there was no change in *him*, but an opening of
my eyes to a side of him that had got lost in the press
of an American holiday. We talked long and came
to the roots of things. And I came to recognise for
the first time the place of the human Jesus in the
Christian world-order.

I saw F. B. later that night. It was about half-
past twelve, and he looked very tired. He was
going to talk with a man. I knew something about
the business ; it was a fight for an almost desperate
soul. He told me something about it, and asked me
to pray for him. I saw from his face what it meant
to him. I think I understood for the first time something of what it meant to Jesus when the three
disciples went to sleep in the garden. I prayed as
never before to the Man of Sorrows, the Revelation
of the loving pity of God.

I did not leave next day. We parted fittingly one
sunny morning among the Bavarian hills, our hearts
full of the splendour of the greatest drama in the
world whose power glows from the faces of the
peasant-players and draws spectators from every
quarter of the world, without distinction of race or
sect. One is a little conscious of the mechanical
triumph of the stage Crucifixion, but in spite of it
there is something there that awakes all the dramatic
instincts in players and spectators, because it appeals
to the most primitive and vital human emotions—
the spectacle of a divine man taking leave of His

friends and going consciously and in full faith to His death.

Since then I have had no occasion to change my mind on this fundamental point. I believe utterly in F. B.'s dictum, which indeed is not F. B.'s— " Look after the Practice and the Theory will look after itself " ; " If any man do My Will, he shall know of the Doctrine." But I do not believe that the two can be permanently kept in water-tight compartments. I have had some interesting experience since then which has increased my distrust of religious short cuts. I do *not* regard as short cuts the essentials of F. B.'s practice—the practice of scrupulous self-discipline as a means of keeping in touch with God and getting into touch with men ; I regard them as necessary preliminaries for finding the way at all. But I believe fundamentally that the world is a process of being saved, of coming gradually through hard work to a knowledge of the Truth, the " Truth which shall make you free." I do not believe in the mechanical repetition of pious formulæ about the Atonement or anything else. That belief may come. My future is uncertain enough. And I do not believe in any religion which shuts the doors of Development.

And F. B. ? He is one of the greatest forces of good in the world at the present time. He is perhaps the most " real live " Christian that I have ever met. . .

CHAPTER IV

A RUGGER BLUE

SHORT, thick-set, with a disproportionate breadth of shoulder, you would never think that this young Irishman had a turn of speed which made him famous at football. Nor on a first acquaintance would you be at all likely to think of him as one who took religion seriously.

A lively mouse-like brown eye lights up a broad good-natured face, while a smile as wide as lips can make it adds constantly a touch of whimsical mental quickness to the mere structural good-nature. He is one who loves lounging in a chair, who wears prodigious woollen waistcoats in winter, who gets his coat into rare disorder whenever he puts his hands in his trouser pockets, who listens lazily, who walks slowly, who speaks with an effort, but who laughs instantly, and with a lighting up of the whole face, at a good retort or a neat witticism, making you feel that he is always on the look-out, gratefully, for occasions of laughter.

I had met him before the house-party came together, and I saw him after the guests of that party had gone their several ways to nearly every quarter of the world. It was, therefore, quite easy for him to tell me his story and to answer my questions.

He said that his father, who is a fine, handsome

Irishman, belongs to those who have a Church and
State religion. It would be impossible for these
people, he said, to imagine a Church without a State.
Their religion is part of their politics, part of their
class feelings. " My father," he related, " never
spoke to me with the least intimacy about religion.
His exhortations consisted of a friendly smack on
the back, accompanied by the admonition, ' Keep
straight, old man,' as if that could do any good to a
fellow up against it. All the same, he was extremely
kind, and a good sportsman. We liked him well
enough."

His mother presents a more difficult problem for
his autobiography. What can he say of her ? To
begin with, she was a wonderful, an altogether ador-
able person—loving beauty, loving fine poetry,
devoted to animals and birds, making God perfectly
real to her children, so that none ever doubted His
existence for a moment ; mystical, too, speaking to
her children of " the Presence of Christ in the midst
of the world," teaching them so convincingly about
that exquisite moral life that they came to think of
religion as " helping others " ; yet, somehow or
other, leaving this son, who adored her, who was
devoted to her, very completely in the dark about
vital matters, leaving him as he says, to find out
things for himself, and to suffer a good deal of
avoidable pain in the process.

" When she spoke about the Presence of Christ,"
he told me, " I hadn't the ghost of an idea what she
meant. I just felt it was something beautiful, like
the sound of wonderful words in the poetry she read
to me. She certainly did succeed in making the idea

of God real to all of us. But it was the idea of a God rather a long way off, and rather overwhelmingly too almighty for our affection. I used to think of Him as One to whom I owed obedience, and who knew what I was doing, and who could be hurt or displeased when I wasn't doing my best. Still, it was a good, useful idea ; and it was mixed up in some way with the beauty of the earth, which we all greatly appreciated, and the wonders of nature, which filled us with a good deal of curious admiration. In this way one had some sort of standard in one's mind, something at least to look up to."

When his moral struggles began, they found him wholly ignorant of their origin and significance. He was a little boy at school, pugilistic and keen on games, cheerful and larky, always ready for springing a joke. This strange black cloud slowly gathering over his mind, darkening the outer world, giving him a haunted feeling inside, troubling his brain and making his heart feel like a bruise—whence did it come, what was its meaning ?

All he knew, by instinct—surely a strange instinct worth thinking about—was that this urge of his being in a particular direction had to be resisted. It was something against him. It was something of which the mere disposition made him ashamed. He felt as if he had been caught doing something underhand. " But the fight was the very devil, and at times I was more than disheartened—I was pretty sick of myself."

This struggle occurred at Rugby. It lessened as he moved up in the school. His last year was passed in a cleaner atmosphere. He never heard one whispered nastiness, never listened to tale or rhyme which could distress him. He was then nearly nineteen years of age, working hard for Cambridge. But the war, which was dragging on into its fourth year, did not come to an end, and away he went to be a soldier. His nineteenth birthday was spent in khaki.

He described this experience of the Army as " a pretty good shock." It taught him for the first time, he told me, " what the world was like." He added with a smile, " Nothing has ever surprised me since that time."

The horror was so great as to be grotesque—as to be comical, laughable. It was like seeing oneself for the first time in a distorting mirror. He cannot help smiling as he speaks of the upside-downness of that moral experience. He found himself among men who were frankly, freely, unfeignedly bad ; who did beastly things with their whole will ; who used the foulest language imaginable because they really relished words with that particular sound ; who never tired of crude stories and dirty limericks ; who were by nature, inclination, and election coarser and more filthy than any animal of the field ; who were by nature, inclination, and election contemptuous of all refinement, all beauty, and all virtue—men whose idea of " a good time " was everything bad, men whose idea of " a bad time " was everything good.

To the Rugby schoolboy this atmosphere was sufficiently repulsive to save him from contamination ; but his natural friendliness to all sorts and conditions of men, his disposition to take life as he finds it and never to set himself in any way above his fellows, might have had ill consequences for his moral peace had he not found in the Army two men as clean-minded and right-hearted as himself. " Religion saw me out," he said ; " but, all the same, one couldn't go through that experience without a change. It made a difference to me."

Released from the Army, he went up to Cambridge. The atmosphere of the University at this time of stir and transition, he found, resembled that of the Army. Undergraduates were soldiers, not schoolboys. But there was a vital difference ; men discussed other things besides vice. In his own set, he told me, " fellows were trying to find a way out." There were discussions on the subject. Some were for cold baths, others for physical exercises, and a few were advocates of developing will-power.

" So far as my own set was concerned," he related, " public opinion was healthy. Men who went up to town for adventures were regarded as contemptible. The long-haired, æsthetic type went in for vice, but the athletic type didn't. In the Army, vice of almost every kind was considered natural. At the Varsity there was a vicious type, and that sort of person was looked upon as a degenerate. The feeling among my set in Cambridge was something like this : We know this is wrong ; how are we to get out of it ? When we succumbed to temptation we were sick with ourselves. But we had sufficient courage to talk the thing over afterwards. We didn't bottle it up, and pretend we kept straight all the time. The thing was too unpleasant for that. We all wanted to be right, and therefore we sometimes discussed over our pipes how we were to dissipate the inclination which clamoured so terrifically for expression. It was with us rather like a discussion about getting fit for a race or a football match. We always looked at it from the point of view of physical fitness. Self-respect came into the matter, although we did not discuss that point of view ; I suppose it was taken for granted ; what came chiefly into the open of our talks was the confounded interruption which this thing introduced into our lives. It was a nuisance, like often catching cold, and a particularly beastly nuisance."

What strikes him in looking back to those days is the strange fact that there was no one to help them. Cambridge is full of churches and clergy, but no aid came from that quarter. The University shepherds altogether ignored this suffering of their flocks. No doctor ever lectured on the subject, no moralist offered a word of advice. The young men were left to fight the matter out among themselves, chiefly in secret.

He does not mean to suggest that particular notice should be paid to this driving temptation of youth ; he is the last person in the world to desire a concentrated attention on such a matter, for that might easily become unhealthy. But he thinks the family doctor should provide the schoolboy with an explanation of this physical disturbance, warning him of the consequences of yielding to its urge and giving him a few notions about cleanliness, physical exercise, and sleep. In particular, he is now persuaded that if religion did its normal work, youth would have absolute power over all temptations that assaulted and hurt the soul, and this without any direct mention of sexual appetite.

While he was at the top of his form as a Rugby football player, as popular a man as ever played for his University, he was overtaken by a serious illness which brought him to death's door. It was impossible for him to face an English winter. He went first to the South of France and often into Italy, reading philosophy for his degree, and sadly lamenting his loss of the Rugger captaincy—a bereavement for which philosophy provided no consolation. In this period of lassitude, weakness, and disappointment, the old enemy awoke and tortured him worse than before.

He returned to Cambridge in order to take his degree, and, still fighting his moral battle, felt nevertheless that he was fighting a lost cause. The attacks were more frequent, the victories fewer. " I don't think," he says, " that I ever actually despaired ; but I certainly had the distinct feeling that I was going downhill—morally, physically, everything. When a fellow gets to the point of feeling that it's not much good fighting he's in a pretty bad way. When he feels that he is going downhill, and that nothing can stop him, he's as good as done for. My state was something like that."

One day, in this pitiful condition of mind, he went to call on a Rugger friend in another college, and there, for the first time in his life, came upon F. B., who made an immediate impression upon him—

the impression of " a good fellow who knew how to put up a fight." They did not speak of religion or of ethics, but the conversation was of such a nature as made our young Irishman feel certain that F. B could help him. When he got up to go he walked over to F. B.'s chair and said to him. " Look here, I'm going to look you up one day." " Do," said F. B., and they parted.

This is how the Rugger Blue tells the rest of the story. " F. B. never pursued me. But I couldn't shake the thought of him out of my mind. I got no line from him, never heard a word about him, never met him. Yet, from that moment of our first meeting, he was hardly ever out of my thoughts. I've talked to other fellows since about their first impressions of F. B., and I find that he took many of them as he took me. It was a strange strong feeling that he really knew about one, and could help one ; that he had the right medicine, and could effect a real cure.

" At last, sure that this feeling was true, and absolutely wretched about myself, I got hold of F. B.'s address and went off to see him. He was out. I wanted to see him so badly that I sat down at the table in his room and began writing him a letter. All of a sudden he bounced into the room, breathlessly. ' I knew there was someone needing me,' he said. It turned out that he was on his way to see somebody else when he felt himself stopped dead in the street and *ordered* to go to his room. The other appointment was important, so he had run all the way back.

" I stayed ten minutes. We never got near what I

wanted to say ; there was a feeling of haste in that
meeting ; but I made it plain that I wanted to have
a talk with him on a private matter, and he promised
to come to my rooms in Trinity on the approaching
Sunday evening.

" That evening was the turning-point in my life.
F. B. arrived between eight and nine. There was a
most beautiful sunset ; the room was filled with its
soft light. He sat with his back to the open window.
I was facing him, looking over the dark outline of his
head to John's Church, with its cross shining against
the glow of the setting sun. It was an extraordinarily
still evening. F. B. seemed to me a part of its still-
ness. He wasn't in one of his cheerful moods. He
hardly said a word, and what he did say was said
in a very subdued tone of voice. I sat looking at the
cross against the sky, wondering how the devil I was
to tell this man, whom I scarcely knew, things about
myself which sickened me, disgraced me in my own
eyes. Somehow or another, I can't tell how it was,
the sight of the cross in the sunset, so high up in that
wonderful air and yet not in the least distant from
my own darkness, gave me a kind of headlong
courage. Before I quite knew what I was doing I
said to him, ' Well, I may as well tell you all about
it.' He said, ' Go on,' and waited for me to continue. I knew then, absolutely, and with a regular
blaze of certainty, that he could clean me out. I
told him the whole trouble, everything.

" I had discussed this thing often enough, but I
had never before confessed it. With other fellows
I had spoken of myself as a physical problem, going
over symptoms. leaving them to infer the actual

tumbles ; but here, for the first time in my life, I had torn up my moral life by the roots and held it out to another man. The feeling of this was not, as I should have thought, one of shame and disgrace, the bitterest humiliation a decent fellow can experience ; on the contrary, it was one of tremendous relief. That in itself surprised me. I had the distinct sensation that one gets in dropping a heavy load from the shoulders—a feeling of expansion and lightness. I remember, too, that I felt as if something which I had kept bottled up inside me ever since I could remember anything was gone, clean gone. You see, I had been feeling fairly desperate, and that made me, once I got started, careless of what I said ; I didn't mind what I told him ; everything came out, everything I loathed and hated in myself, and in coming out it seemed to stay out.

" F. B. never spoke a word. I couldn't see his face against the light, and I couldn't tell how he was taking it, and I don't think I very much cared. I wound up in a natural way by telling him that I'd tried athletics, that I'd gone in for all sorts of exercises, cold baths, and tricks for strengthening the will, but in vain. I was going downhill in my thought life ; what was I to do? Did he know a cure ? Would he advise me ?

" Then F. B. told me everything."

Three particulars in that " everything " seemed to have brought instant illumination to the mind of this undergraduate. First, that moral chaos is inevitable when there is no singleness of mind ; second, that the power which purifies, strengthens, and upholds can only become real to those who long for it, and open the doors of their cleansed hearts to receive it in silence ; and third, that no soul, truly conscious of that power, can be satisfied with its own salvation. "If you sit still," he said, "it's hopeless ; help other men."

That was the supreme test. A man could easily prove for himself whether he had genuine singleness of mind, genuine contact with the divine power. All he had to do was to consider his attitude towards other men. Did he want to help others ? Had he something in himself which could help them ? It was no use pretending in this matter. No help could come to a soul that didn't really want it. No purity could come to a heart that prayed for it, " but not yet." No power could come into a life that was selfish.

" Sin blinds, and sin binds." Be careful Think those two words over—*blinds* and *binds*. Don't be quite sure that what you think you see is the truth. Don't be quite sure that you can really do what you like. Cross-examine yourself. You may be blind. You may be a slave. While sin is in your mind you are not a free creature, you are not a seeing creature. Sin is self : while it is there in the mind, whatever form it takes, a man may deceive himself to his life's end, may even go so far as to believe that he is good, that he is serving God, that he is helping other men. But he isn't. Sin walls God out. " Then will I profess unto them, I never knew you." An awful sincerity, a sincerity that searches every crack and corner of the human heart, is necessary if God is to enter—the living and the Eternal Righteousness.

Many believe that when they pray for purity they really and truly want to be pure. They deceive themselves. It is a mere passing emotion. The root of the sin is still in their hearts. Two things must go together—a deep and passionate hatred of sin, a deep and passionate craving for God.

Ask—with singleness of mind—and it shall be given you ; seek—with singleness of desire—and ye shall find ; knock—with singleness of purpose—and it shall be opened unto you. A good tree cannot bring forth evil fruit, neither can a corrupt tree bring forth good fruit.

The reasonableness, the inexorable justice of this teaching, brought instant illumination to the soul of the young Irishman, and he took that plunge away from self which baptises the spirit of a man in the living waters of eternal life. He really wanted the touch that makes personality a whole.

He said to me that so wonderful was his belief that he set about " tackling other men " almost at once. He told those men what F. B. had told him, and recommended them to try what he himself was trying, F. B.'s method of rising early in the morning to be alone and silent with the thought of God in the soul. He told them that in these times of silence he had learned to relax his whole body, and that with so simple an invitation as, " God, come into my soul, and help me," evil thoughts drained clean out of him, and he really did become vitally conscious of invisible power.

All this he did in so masculine and sincere a fashion that a group soon formed in his room of men who really longed for spiritual life—a life which they could not find in the formal ritual, however beautiful, of churches and chapels. F. B., who realised the remarkable power of this man to influence others, soon afterwards sent him over to Oxford, where his twin brother was at Balliol, in order to begin there a similar work of personal religion.

The Balliol brother invited a few men to his room and the Cambridge brother talked to them. One of these men came from Christ Church ; he was impressed, and suggested a somewhat bigger gathering at the House.

" It was there," says the Rugger Blue, smiling, "that I made my first speech. It was pretty rotten. The room was full of scholars, and I felt as nervous as a cat. But after I had got through they took the matter up in discussion, and we debated it from pretty nearly every angle till the small hours. What struck them most, I think, was the reasonableness of F. B.'s idea that the measure of help is the measure of desire. They never flinched or jibbed at this idea because it is just. Theological difficulties were hardly mentioned ; the centre of discussion was how to get the heart honest in its desire for the right thing. We talked and talked till the moon was high in the sky. Then we went out into the Quad, and walked round and round the fountain, still talking. I had a fellow on each arm. Sharing a trouble makes friends. The feeling that you can help another fellow is one of the best in the world. We were tremendously happy. They came to see me in my rooms. We made a compact which still holds good. Wonderful things have come of that visit."

Later on, during the Long Vacation, the Rugger Blue arranged a house-party in Cambridge, so that a number of men should meet F. B. and discuss the whole question of personal religion.

He gave me a characteristic account of that gathering. " I don't suppose I've got much of a reputation for tact," he said, smiling broadly ; " in any case, I never stopped to think how the people I asked would mix. The thing was to get a lot of interesting fellows together, and leave F. B. to do the rest. The consequence was we had a party of thirty men—Indians, Yanks, Japanese, Chinese, Oxford, Cambridge, business men, Members of Parliament, and one or two howling swells from the War Office. It was most amusing. You saw Etonians in white spats talking to prospective socialistic curates ! And there was extraordinary cordiality. Everyone was interested. It seemed as if they had all been life-friends. I never knew such a lack of strain in any gathering of men. We kept it up for several days. We got right down to bedrock—the need for absolute uncompromising, all-out sincerity. And I'm perfectly certain of this, that every man there was helped. Out of that party grew the party you came to ; and we've got another coming on in a month's time at Cambridge ; and after that some of us are going to Universities in Germany, and some to Universities in the United States."

The last time I saw him was at Talbot House, in York Road, Lambeth, happy in the midst of very lively youth. He has decided to be a doctor, and when he has taken his medical degree he is going to attach himself to the Talbot House Movement, placing himself and his services entirely at the disposal of that very noble fellow, P. B. Clayton, M.C., the adored chaplain of Poperinghe, to do what he can to help young men through every illness of soul and body.

CHAPTER V

WHEN the house-party gathered together he was crossing the Atlantic, but long before he arrived the English garden in which we walked and debated grew well used to the sound of his name. I was assured that he was "an absolute topper." I was told that everybody loved him. Again and again he figured as the hero of a tale or the author of a good saying. The mention of his name always brought affectionate smiles to the faces of those who knew him.

Thus dangerously heralded, P. G., as I shall call him for brevity's sake and anonymity's sake, joined our party on the day before it broke up. I had the pleasure of hearing him make one very simple and modest speech, and the greater pleasure of taking a moonlight walk with him under the tall trees of that beautiful garden. We agreed together that he should pay me a visit in Dorsetshire before he returned to America. He kept that promise, taking my family by storm, and leaving behind him an impression which is still as gracious and fresh as the hour which brought him into our circle.

His gift of charm, I think, lies in a wholly unconscious retention of the graces of boyhood. There is no hardness in his character, no sense of firmness in his disposition, no hint of decisive energy in his mind. If he were a writing-man, Macaulay would frighten him and Lamb would be very dear to him. Among the dogmatists he would be all at sea ; among the men of " push and go " he would be trodden underfoot. He suggests to you that his mind is still full of wonder, like the mind of a child.

The memories of his defeats have left no bitterness ; the remembrance of his victories has brought no sense of triumph. His pilgrim's progress, I think, has something of the radiance and innocence that we find in Bunyan's page. Everything in his nature is modest, gentle, and sincere. He is in this world as a shy boy must be accounted one of the guests at a roystering party. You feel that he will never quite settle down, never come to feel that all this bustle and stir are in the true nature of reality. He sees something that the rest of us do not see, but is afraid to talk about it, lest he draw attention to himself. He makes you think of Mr. Dick without his delusion, or of William Blake without his insanity. Every motion of his spirit is the expression of a profound and incorruptible simplicity—a simplicity so wholly unconscious that it makes everybody love him. Nothing in the least theatrical has ever brushed even the outskirts of his mind.

He spent his boyhood in a small American country town, characterised by all the respectabilities and pruderies of a thoroughly compromising civilisation, entirely without the inspiration of the great realities.

He was one of three children, and the only son. Between father and son, so far as religion was concerned, there was a wall, but between son and mother no obstacle of any kind. He believed everything she told him, and saw nothing in her life to criticise or to disturb his worship. She was orthodox, but not narrow-minded ; he loved her completely.

The first incident in his spiritual life occurred when his elder sister, seven years older than himself, returned from college with a definite religious experience. This change in his sister enabled him to comprehend the difference between " first-hand and second-hand religion." He describes the change in his sister as the change from sleep to waking. Something of the same nature occurred in himself ; he was no longer asleep, but could not feel himself properly awake.

One thing greatly struck him in this transitional condition of mind—the visible fact that his sister's life was now " propagating in the lives of other people." This seemed to him a very wonderful thing, and the thought that it was possible for one person to make another person happy, to make an indifferent person active, and a bad person good, stuck in his mind.

But, though he took part in the religious activities of his school, he found that he didn't fit, that he wasn't in the least like his sister, and therefore he came to the conclusion that he was not yet properly awake. This idea of sleep and waking came to him with the simple naturalness characteristic of all his thinking. It was not an idea put into his mind by somebody else. He came of himself to think of people as asleep, half-asleep, half-awake, awake, broad-awake.

He seems to have passed through boyhood without

moral disturbance of any kind. His one distress was the haunting thought that he could not establish a more real relation with the God of orthodox religion. But this thought was without distress. It rose into consciousness between periods of singular happiness, for he was a boy made for the delights of school-days.

His battle began in his first term at college. He went to Yale, which is in New Haven, and for the first time in his life breathed the atmosphere of a town which had the flavour of a great city. All the placid provincialism of the little country town in which he had dreamed and mused away the years of boyhood was consumed in the rakish gaiety of this University town. A walk down Chapel Street was enough to set his head spinning. This street, with its fashionable shops, its numerous theatres, and its cosmopolitan restaurants, is a favourite parade for harlots and " adventure girls "—pretty girls from the chorus of comic operas, and girls of the town whose moral standards are on the same level as their standards in manners, literature, and art. The effect it makes on a provincial is one of rebuke ; he is persuaded to feel that he is narrow, dull, wanting in spirit, a prisoner to fear, a captive of stupidity. The bright people smiling and laughing in the sunshine of that cheerful thoroughfare seem to flaunt a superior liberty and a higher courage in the dazed eyes of the youthful provincial. They are not the victims of illusion ; it is he, gaping at them, who is deceived. They are not going down to perdition ; but he wanting to join, and yet afraid, is on the road to mediocrity.

Nothing in the religion of this boy was proof

against the temptations of Chapel Street. For the
first time in his life he experienced an uprush of
those feelings which are so powerful to create the
highest happiness of the human soul, so powerful
to destroy the last rags of its liberty and self-respect.
He was tempted, and the temptation seemed to foul
his spirit. He could not withstand the call of
apparent beauty and apparent gladness.

This tremendous pressure on his purity drove him to
religion as a refuge. He describes it as a home to fly
to while he was at college; a narcotic which brought
relief; an argument, a persuasion, but not light.

On his way home at the end of his first term he
passed through New York. There was a great storm
crashing over the city, and he watched it with his
thoughts set on his own burden. That burden, he
says, was awful. He asked himself, Why isn't Christ
personal to me? and in asking that question a sigh
broke from his lips, and with the escape of that sigh
something of his burden seemed to go. He felt that
he had begun to get an answer.

When he returned to Yale it was with the decision
to follow his sister's example, and " to propagate
in other lives." The experience was disheartening.
One of the students was very ill, perhaps dying, and
P. G. went to see him. They talked together, but
" I couldn't get through to him," he says; " there
were barriers between us as big as mountains."

He spoke of another man he tried to influence.
" This man," he said, " belonged to the type of
attractive sinner—a delightful person, a man with
personality; charming, with magic about him,

lovable. He was intellectual, and could floor my persuasions with arguments gathered from history and human experience and science. He was quite friendly ; he knew I cared for him ; I think he liked me ; and he was the kind of man who appreciated sympathy ; but nothing I could say made the smallest difference to him. You see, what I was doing was to try to superimpose myself on other people ; I was trying to do them good from a height on which I wasn't really standing. That is fatal."

Intellectual difficulties presented themselves. Orthodox religion was exposed to the attacks of clever young men who knew more science than theology. There were, indeed, intellectual courses at the college which seemed to him directed against religion. He was shaken, but he suffered no mental anguish. Involved in theological disputes, he had nothing to say. He retired from them to read his Bible more industriously and to pray more earnestly for light.

His sympathy with men took him into all quarters. One night he found himself in a room full of rackety students, who presently began to tell coarse stories. P. G. rebuked them, opposed himself single-handed to the whole group. " I was dealing with symptoms, not causes," he relates, with a smile ; " instead of opposing myself to the group, I ought to have waited and reasoned with individuals."

He had now made up his mind to attach himself to the Christian Student Movement in India. Temptation had eased. Prayer meant much more to him than it had ever meant in the past. Religion had at

Dc

last become apparently real. Yet a trouble remained which preyed upon his peace of mind.
" Religion was real to me," he says, " but I could
not give it away."

He left the University and went out to India.
For three years, loving his work, he remained in that
country, forming, as he says, superficial friendships,
but doing nothing really effective to stop the appal-
ling vice which existed among young Indians.

He returned to America, and joined the famous
seminary at Hartford, Connecticut. For a year he
was profoundly happy. He loved his freedom, the
peace of the seminary, and the long, unbroken hours
of study. He thought he was fitting himself to be
a teacher of the Christian religion.

The second year brought disillusion, and something akin to terror. Temptations assaulted him
with a quite incredible force, a quite sickening per-
sistency. Doubt, too, was for ever whispering to his
conscience. He found that his heart was full of impurity, his mind as full of intellectual dishonesty.
He was hedging, compromising, pretending. Rather
than cause pain to others he felt that he must go on
with the religious life ; but it began to be to him a
shadow, a phantasm, something out of a forgotten
past that had no meaning for a present terribly and
overwhelmingly insistent.

He said to me, " I really do not know any form
of mental misery so tragic as the misery of the theological student—the afflicted disciple. The men in
these colleges and seminaries are the hungriest
groups in the world. They have good motives, but
no direction They are assailed by temptations

which make them ashamed. They do things which choke them with a sense of self-contempt, a sense of hypocrisy. The atmosphere is more corrupting and damning than the atmosphere of Universities. One feels that these places are full of repression, full of unuttered sin. There's something furtive about them. You don't get public drunkenness, public gambling, public immorality. There's no visible and healthy clash of good and evil. Good is taken for granted, and absence of evil is also taken for granted. But the evil is there ; and the good—well, it is not easy to feel its influence. As for the professors, their only experience of religion is a memory. They tell the students what happened years ago, not what happened coming down in the tram, or in the home last night. They have no reality for these desperate students, who spend half their time studying the soul-killing controversies of long-ago theologies, and the other half in fighting temptations sharp as steel. People wonder at drunkenness and ' rags ' among Varsity men ; I think I know how those things come about. They are attempts to break away from repression, to escape from a maddening sense of conflicting duality."

One of the students at Hartford had been a miner and a sailor ; he had made a fortune and spent it. He was about thirty-five years of age, and used to write sermons for the other students. He had a gift for preaching which created admiration among the younger men. P. G. liked this strange man and talked to him, tried to " get below the surface to the place where he lived." One day the ex-miner said to him, " Shall I tell you what I am ? I'm a damned hypocrite. I've been twice with women quite lately."

P. G. had the terror always before his eyes that he too might fall. One night in New York he had to rush into the streets and walk as hard as he could go for miles, fearing that the temptation would beat him. He says, " I was a divided personality. There were two of me ; no unity. I felt that I might fall ; yet I felt that nothing on earth should make me."

He was in this state of mind, seeing little hope before him of avoiding hypocrisy, when F. B. came to Hartford as an Extension Lecturer. His subject was, " How to deal with Other Men ; how to get into their Lives." One day P. G. was walking in the grounds of the college when someone, coming up from behind, took his arm, and said, " This is P. G., isn't it ? " P. G. turned to find F. B. at his side, smiling in the far-away manner which sometimes takes the place of his usual alertness. He began to speak of someone in India who had met P. G.

The immediate feeling of P. G. was one of conviction that he could speak with complete frankness and confidence to this stranger—stranger no longer, for the touch of his hand had conveyed an instant feeling of friendliness.

" I knew," he told me, " that here was a man of understanding sympathy, one who wouldn't be shocked, one who could help. Another thing I knew—that there was no professionalism about him, that he wouldn't think of me as ' a case,' that he was a genuine man genuinely interested in another man. I remember, too, I had the feeling that in this man there was plenty of time. Nothing suggested commercial bustle. He seemed to me to be living in a wonderful spiritual leisure. We parted with nothing much said between us, but on the following day, after breakfast, he came and sat with me on the garden steps in the morning sun. For the first time in my life I told another man exactly how I stood, and something of what I had suffered. I turned to him and said, ' My mind is filled with a cloud of evil thoughts ; why do I have these evil thoughts ? ' To my astonishment he said at once, ' Why, P. G., I have those evil thoughts,' as if he were surprised that they should worry me. Directly he said that I had the feeling he knew what to do with them. There was a deep sense of relief in my mind. He said nothing more to help me. All he added was that I must come to see him later in the day. But I felt extraordinarily happy, just as if the fight was over.

" When we came to have our talk he told me that the reason I was tortured was simply because I was fighting temptation direct. The attempt at repression was the cause of my suffering. It was necessary for me to leave all such fatal egoism and to get out into the lives of other men—altruism, Christianity. He spoke quietly and convincingly. But I wanted it my own way, and comfortable ; I didn't want to pay the price ; so I challenged him to tell me why I could not get relief in the old way, by prayer and reading the Bible. He told me that I had to get into the lives of other men, and that was all there was to it. Selfishness was my sin. I wasn't thinking of others.

" One day, shortly after this, I was walking in

town with him when we came across two drunken
men. He told me to take one while he took the
other. I was paralysed by fear. I hid behind a
telegraph-post. But F. B. collared his man and saw
him home. Next day, in the midst of a meeting,
F. B. had an irresistible impulsion to go out into the
street ; someone there wanted him. He left the
meeting, went out into the street, and there was the
drunken man of last night. F. B. put that man on
the right road.

" When he told me this I felt poverty-stricken.
Religion began to seem to me something that was not
natural. I should never be able to handle other men
as F. B. handled them. I was like a young surgeon
with trembling knife confronting a new operation.

" I confessed this feeling to F. B., and he took me a
step further ; he taught me the principles of religion.
He explained that I felt helpless because my religion
was not in action. This meant that I had never
experienced ' the expulsive power of a new affection.' If I had real love for men I should be willing
to share my temptations with them, to confess to
them my secret thoughts, to get alongside of their
souls, to work with them and for them to the end of
redemption. Every man, he said, could test the
reality of his religion by finding out whether he would
make sacrifices to help others.

" I saw what he meant intellectually, but I didn't
want to come to it. I told myself that there was
something immodest in his suggestion, that my
spiritual life was too sacred to talk about—as if
anything is too sacred that helps other men ! So I
withstood him.

" One day he surprised me very much by saying that he was going back to China for six months and wanted me to go with him. I had another year to run at Hartford. China did not attract me. I'm not sure that F. B. attracted me. I rather shrank from his too personal methods. But he persuaded me, and those six months stretched into two years, and those two years are the happiest memories in my life.

" Before I left Hartford I decided to try F. B.'s method. I went to a theological student who seemed to me to be troubled, to be suffering, and confessed to him my own secret sin—impurity. The feeling of relief was extraordinary. The student came to life, confessed his secret sin to me, and ended our talk by saying, ' Prayer is going to mean something now ; the Bible is going to mean something now.' To both of us it seemed that religion had never been real to us before, never been alive, and that now it was the very biggest thing alive.

" The revelation came to me in this conviction : *God floods in when a man is honest.* I had been looking at religion from the intellectual point of view. I had never really seen it as the supreme power of morality. I had never really apprehended that religion redeems and dominates the sinful heart of man—not merely the sin of impurity, but the entire moral life—selfishness and all our moral hesitancies.

" I came to myself in confessing to another man, that is to say in being perfectly honest. For the first time in my life I felt that there was no pretence in my soul, that another man whom I wanted to help knew me as I knew myself, and that I really and truly did want to help him—that I had torn away all pretensions in order that I might be able to help him.

" I am convinced that confession plays a tremendous part in religious life. I don't think it is too much to say that until a man confesses his sin to another man he can never really be spiritually vital. One knows scores of men who carry guilty consciences, and who think they square accounts by confessing their sins in secret to God, and genuinely trying not to commit those sins again. Such men can never help another ; such men haven't the ghost of an idea what redemption means. They pretend. Their religion is a form. Their life is a dead letter.

" An interesting story occurs to me. A friend of mine wanted very much to help a particular friend of his who was involved in some trouble with a girl. He tried and tried, in vain. He asked me why he couldn't do this thing. He wasn't lacking in sympathy ; he wanted to help his friend ; why couldn't he ? I got him to go over his past life. He found that there was an unconfessed sin on his conscience. As a schoolboy he had stolen money from his father. It was a hard task, but he went to his father and confessed his sin. The result was not only ability to help his friend but a real pentecostal joy in his own heart. He said to me, ' Now I'm ready to go all the way in this thing.' How simply a man can be born again ! One act of honesty. Reality ! "

Let me interrupt the narrative for a moment to remind the reader that in Morton Prince's *The*

Unconscious many stories showing that some forgotten incident in the past, but not forgotten by the unconscious mind, may prey upon physical health and even be the cause of serious physical ills.

I remember one case in particular. A woman subject to epileptic fits was hypnotised by Dr. Prince, and taken back by him through all the days of her life in search for the shock which had deranged her mental processes. He discovered from her unconscious mind that once, as a little girl, she had been sitting alone in her nursery with a kitten in her lap, that this kitten had suddenly had a fit, that she had screamed for her nurse, terrified by the kitten, and that the nurse did not come for a very long time. The doctor awakened her from hypnosis, told her of this incident, of which she had no memory, and so disposed of the cause of her trouble. From this case it will be seen that even things which the conscious mind has forgotten may remain in the folds of being, festering the entire life.

Religion, one may observe, seems to have known by instinct what painful science is only now beginning to suspect. Always it has taught the need of confession, restitution, and a cleansed heart.

P. G., at any rate, is insistent on the power of confession to fill the spirit with an entirely new sense of life. He lays all his emphasis there. To him the matter is not in the least mysterious. Confession is merely a sign of an absolute honesty within, a sign that the long attempt to compromise and equivocate is over, a sign that the personality is at last unified, not divided, a sign that the soul really means what it says, and truly believes what it has hitherto only professed or tried to believe.

By confession he means no formal act of clericalism, performed to square accounts with the Deity, but a most personal act on the part of one man to another—particularly to the man one is trying to help—an act that attests honesty and brings one man close to another, in sympathy and reality.

He is the more certain of the power of confession from his experience in the East. He told me that he found he could do nothing with men in China, Japan, and Korea until he persuaded them to confess their secret sins, but that directly this confession was made they experienced precisely the same joyous relief which he had experienced. The confessions of young men in China, Japan, and Korea, he says, fit perfectly in with the confessions of young men in England and America. He agrees with F. B., " Crows are black the whole world over."

" I saw many miracles in the East," he said to me, " and I am now seeing like miracles in America and in England. All the world over sin is darkening men's lives, and hypocrisy is paralysing the power of religion to save them. Religion is a universal force. It does not much matter, I think, what theological language is used to express the immense miracle of redemption. What matters is making it real to suffering men that directly they are absolutely honest in desiring release from the slavery of sin, God will flood into their hearts, and they really will be born again. Redemption *cannot* come, I'm perfectly certain of this, until the heart is so hungry

for it that it will confess everything to another. One
has to be awfully real oneself to experience reality.

" I remember a strange incident in China. I came
across, in one of the mission colleges, a Chinese
teacher who was a complete hypocrite. He drank,
he gambled, and he had relations with married
women. He was a man of some intellect and no little
power. One night, sitting over the fire, he said to me,
' All this Christianity is a legend. Jesus, you know, is
not an historical figure. I never say my prayers. I
teach, because I can teach. But,' with a shrug of
his shoulders, ' I do not believe what I teach.' I took
no notice of his effort to get me into a theological
argument. I spoke of the Christ of universal human
experience, the Christ who saves, the Christ who
redeems, the Christ who had made all the difference
to me. He turned, with a strange light in his eyes,
looking at me over his shoulder, his hands still
extended to the fire, and ' How would I take that
medicine ? ' he asked. I said to him, ' Will you pray
from your heart, " Jesus, if there be a Jesus, I want
you to clean me up " ? ' To my surprise, then and
there, looking into the fire, he prayed that prayer.
Then he got up and left me. The next day he came
to me and said, ' You know, this thing works
marvellously.' It was his first experience of personal religion. He had never before seen redemption
as the central fact of Christianity. He said to me,
' Now I feel on top.' He had never before looked at
religion as a real power that enters the heart, changes
the life, and gives a new birth to the soul. I am quite
sure he had never wanted to be cleaned up.

" What strikes me most in all these wonderful

experiences—for it is a wonderful thing to see a man born again—is their extreme simplicity. Directly a man is really honest the miracle occurs. Many deceive themselves. They protest that they want to be rid of sin, and it isn't really true. Others do want to be rid of their sin, but selfishly, for their own ease, their own self-respect, or because they are afraid of being found out. Those find it difficult. But when a man hungers and thirsts to be rid of sin so that he may help others, it really is extraordinary how soon the step is taken from darkness to light, from sleep to waking. It seems natural and right, when one considers that the message of Jesus was unselfishness. There can't be any vital experience of religion where selfishness has got a hold, whatever form it takes. What surprises one is not the miracle of conversion, but the ease with which even very good men will go on deceiving themselves all their life long ; men who are moral and philanthropic, but with some root of selfishness in their hearts, which prevents them from ever experiencing a new birth or saving a man who is lost. Why do these people deceive themselves ? It seems such a mad idea, attempting to hoodwink God. I suppose they are not properly awake, that they don't understand what they are doing."

Few of the followers of F. B. exercise so great an influence over others as this gracious person whose voice and smile, could I convey them to this " brutish paper," would endear him to the reader and give a deeper meaning to his words.

I spoke to him a little of theological difficulties.

He admitted those difficulties, and agreed that they will have to be faced ; but he said, very modestly and unpretentiously, that redemption would remain the central truth of religious life whatever might be the future language of theology.

" There is no fact so great in the experience of men," he said quietly, " as the fact that a soul on the extreme edge of destruction can be redeemed to life merely by turning round—sincerely turning right round."

The most beautiful of all the parables certainly teaches that the Father can do nothing until the son has turned his face homewards.

CHAPTER VI

BEAU IDEAL

CONSPICUOUS in the house-party for his good looks was a man well known at Eton and Oxford, whom we will here call Beau Ideal. Over six feet, with a fresh boyish complexion, clear bright eyes, thick fair hair very carefully brushed, a clipped moustache, and something a little dandiacal about his clothes, this young Hercules of twenty-four English summers looked exactly like the circulating library's idea of an officer in the Brigade of Guards.

I noticed that while he lounged in a deep chair, speaking with a tired drawl, as though discussion bored him, he was activity itself when he got upon his feet. One caught sight of him at times in voluminous flannels and coarse-knitted sweater hurrying away to get an hour's tennis ; or missed him from the luncheon table to learn that he had gone off to play in a cricket match. Sometimes it seemed to me that behind his boyish handsomeness there smouldered the flames of a once difficult temper. But the chief impression he made on one's mind was that of the perfectly healthy, sport-loving, and well-bred young Briton at his topmost best. Whether he had brains was another matter. How he came to be interested in religion puzzled me a good deal.

He amused me one night by an answer he made to

a challenging question by F. B. The Surgeon of
Souls had been contrasting, with a deep and rather
reproachful seriousness, the way in which the movement for personal religion was spreading in the
Universities of the United States with that movement in the British Isles. He said it was up to
English Varsity men to see that much more energy
was put into this work ; what did they propose to
do about it ? (Silence.) What suggestions had they
to make ? (Silence.) Surely some of them had at
least a part of an idea in their minds.

After some slow-dragging moments of nervous
silence, Beau Ideal, sprawling in a big chair, lazily
made answer, " If you told Oxford men that an
Oxford man wanted to talk to them about religion
they wouldn't pay the smallest attention to you,
beyond a glance to see if you were drunk or off your
head. But I believe there is another University in
England ; if I remember rightly, at a place called
Cambridge ; and I rather think that if you told
Oxford men a fellow from this extraordinary place
wanted to speak to them they'd go, even if it was to
hear about religion, just out of curiosity to see what
manner of animal Cambridge produces."

In this way, rousing the Cambridge men of the
party to intellectual reprisals, Beau Ideal made a
valuable contribution to the debate. Behind the
persiflage was an idea, and within the irony a truth.

Seldom have I been more out of my reckoning with
a human being than I presently found myself in the
case of this handsome young giant. He came to see
me in London, and alone together I discovered that

he was not merely interested in religion as a possible theory of existence, but that he was truly consumed with a fervorous passion for all those intellectual and moral sacrifices which orthodox religion so obviously calls upon a man to make. Instead of a dandy I had caught a fanatic.

His manner completely changed. There was the same lounging disposition of the big body, but no drawl in the speech, no sleepy languor of the eyelids. Indeed, there were moments when quite visibly he became electric, and had to put restraint on his enthusiasm ; moments when his quick and eager words broke suddenly down, and a blush of misgiving came into his face, a look of inquiry darting from his eyes, as though the mind would discover whether it was not prejudicing its case by moral emotionalism. Wonderful to relate, Beau Ideal is a genuine firebrand.

From boyhood, I learned, he has had the greatest difficulty in bridling a hot temper. The sound of a voice could irritate him, an ugly fashion in clothes make him hate the wearer, an opinion with which he did not agree rouse in him an impulse almost homicidal. He has tramped many miles over the highlands merely to escape from people. He has sailed and fished for days only as an excuse to flee from society that rubbed him the wrong way. Games, which he plays with tremendous vigour, were the chief outlet in his boyhood for irritable energies boiling up within him to the fever point of exasperation.

When he went to Christ Church he was still first and foremost an athlete, but there was a disposition in him to scholarship, and he was soon regarded as an undergraduate with an intellectual future. He found the tentative, superior, and philosophical temperament of Oxford entirely to his liking. His set in the House was the best of its time. It was composed of men who took themselves seriously, but were careful not to let it be thought that they took themselves too seriously. In this set Beau Ideal, by grace of body and charm of mind, was a figure of some eminence.

His thoughts were occupied chiefly by politics and philosophy. He contracted an interest for social problems. The world appeared to him as a diverting problem providing endless opportunities for delightful theories—a serious problem, but a problem all the better for being regarded with a certain irony of outlook.

Across this intellectual life ran the interrupting diagonal of a sex pride. He knew very well that he was a rather out-of-the-way good-looking person. He liked to notice the effect he produced on entering a ballroom. It pleased him immensely that the prettiest girls, wherever he went, gave him special glances and wanted him very much to dance with them. He showed no outward sign of this pardonable vanity ; indeed, he assumed an intentional modesty to aggravate the effect of his charm ; but inwardly he was about as full of foppish conceit as any " lady's man " that ever lived.

So his days were passing, not innocent of feverish sin, but chiefly taken up with philosophy, games, dancing, and affairs of the wardrobe, when one summer's night he was introduced to F. B. in Peck

Quad. F. B. suggested that they should take a walk round the Quad, and began to ask Beau Ideal what he was thinking about. Beau Ideal began to speak about life in general—his interest in eugenics, birth control, the problems of population, and the chief social difficulties of the time.

All of a sudden F. B. said to him : " Those things aren't disturbing you. You know what's robbing you of peace, don't you ? " And, then and there, as Beau Ideal puts it, he began " stirring up the mud."

It was a beautiful, still summer night, with pale stars above the roofs of the college, the moon coming up in a mist of silver, the sound of the ancient city at that late hour little more than a far-distant sea-murmur. Beau Ideal could hear his heart beating as he listened to the trenchant words of this inexplicable man walking at his side ; he could feel his cheeks colouring in the cool air as the mud stirred up by the American got into the circulation of his blood and mounted to his conscience. Never before had a man spoken to him as this man was now speaking.

Left to himself, with a disturbed consciousness and a guilty conscience, Beau Ideal tried in vain to take up the threads of his former life. F. B. had said something to him which made the fact of sin a towering and menacing fact of human life. He could not escape from the thought that all the social and political problems with which he had hitherto amused his intellect—problems convenient enough as topics of conversation—were so many molehills in comparison with this single mountainous fact of human sin. Discussions with some of his friends who had gone rather deeper into this same great matter with the American Surgeon of Souls presently led Beau Ideal to lend the light of his countenance to the proceedings of the Christian Student Movement in Christ Church. He was careful from the first to make it understood that his interest in that movement was social and political. Where that movement was concerned with issues worthy the attention of an intellectual man of the world, there our young god was willing to appear in the Roman garments of a Mecænas. As to anything so contrary to the established customs of good breeding as personal discussions concerning the hypothetical relations of an unproved soul with a theoretical God, clearly in that respect nothing could be expected of him.

But F. B. had stirred up the mud so effectually that when he was alone by himself Beau Ideal was far too conscious of his own personal sins—not other people's sins—for peace of mind. Instead of the boyish irritability which had once made such a turmoil of his days he found himself now assailed by a profound and morbid unrest of soul which robbed him of peace and dogged every step of his happiness.

To be rid of such a tax on his patience he played games harder than ever, and harder than ever applied himself to a study of philosophy. It seemed to him that with a healthy mind in a healthy body he would presently be able not only to form a satisfactory thesis of existence, but to get rid of certain bad habits which he did not doubt degraded him.

But the unrest continued. It continued till he found himself confronted by a choice, which he calls the choice between philosophy or religion. Either he had to remain outside the struggle of man's soul, looking on at it with interest, patience, tolerance, and a calming irony, or he had to take a plunge into a quite other fount and cleanse himself of that which fouled him, body and soul.

All his inclinations were towards philosophy ; all his heredity was against religion.

In this frame of mind he went away to Sark, on purpose to fight the matter out with himself and by himself. It happened that one day, sitting on a rock in a high wind, with a great and staggering sea breaking in vast commotion against that ironbound coast, so that he was drenched with spindrift and swayed by the gale, this problem resolved itself into one clear question which thus presented itself to his mind :

Is it true, or untrue, that philosophy, regarded as a mathematical system of thought, fails to provide an adequate answer to the question propounded by a system within it, namely ethics, as to *how* a man is to live according to his highest lights—or, as Aristotle would say, κατα τον ὀρθον λογόν, according to right reason ?

He began his answer by confessing that a man does not need philosophy to teach him what is right and what is wrong. Philosophy is unnecessary to tell a man what he should do in the sphere of conduct. Within the man himself, born with him into this world, an inherent part of his nature, perhaps as old as the first movement of evolution, is a disposition towards his best, at any rate a recognition that there is a best and that there is a worst.

Then he saw that human progress—that is to say, human happiness and human freedom—had chiefly depended on man's response to this movement within him—this movement in the direction of the best which had so often in the history of humanity involved the supreme sacrifice.

At this point he asked himself what part philosophy had played in that struggle. Many great philosophers had elevated man to a noble dignity by the exercise of purely rational faculties, but what part had philosophy itself played in freeing the multitude from the tyranny of evil habits and ennobling the moral character of the human race?

His own experience told him that philosophy is often employed to blind men's eyes to the real issues, to find an excuse for delinquency, to explain away a cancer of moral life, to justify in theory practices which the conscience of the individual tells him to be wrong. The moral life of Plato—who cares to think about it? Acton's intellectual contempt for those who would find in climate or in chronology an excuse for evil—how justifiable! Plausible explanations, how often is this the work of philosophy in action!

Another idea presented itself to his mind. Philosophy gives man a false notion of liberty by challenging all rules and refusing to recognise the

authority of, or the reverence due to, anything which
is not explicable to the contemporary reason. It
destroys all standards save those of its own time and
its own creation. It is the declared enemy of humble
faith. It will not take for granted even the most
sacred intuitions of the human soul. It is incompatible with earnest moral endeavour. In nearly all
its aspects it is destructive and negative.

Such, he tells me, were the thoughts thrown up by
the ocean under the stern cliffs of Sark—thoughts no
less numerous, troubled and jumbled than the waves
of that disordered sea.

The battle, of course, was only half fought. He
was left merely with the ruins of a boy's faith in
philosophy as a breakwater against humanity's sea
of troubles.

"It is the prerogative of youth, I suppose," he
wrote to me of that time, "to rail against things as
they are, and in those days I shared keenly in that
dissatisfaction, and included myself among the least
satisfactory phenomena. The failure of materialism
came to me as a profound conviction ; and, against
that, the necessity to make use of spiritual force. It
became clear that the only ultimate significance in
life was genuine moral effort. I suppose the appeal
came most directly as a question of the general welfare and happiness of people. They themselves had
failed to promote their own welfare. What must be
done ? "

A little later he was able to say : " Even the most
superficial study of the Christian religion was enough
to show me that in the sophisticated atmosphere of

modern times, in a welter of sex psychology and necromancy of nearly every kind, an age of few restraints and no reverences, an age with no holy of holies for ' the unsanctified curiosities of common men,' the simple ethic of Jesus would work a healthy change. Honesty in commerce, sincerity in the Church, sympathy between employer and employed, purity and decency in social life, idealism and earnestness in political life—what a change would such things effect ! *Pari passu* with these things came the challenge of one's own conscience—the searching thought of one's own personal morality. I heard a friend say of Dr. Arnold of Rugby, ' He was old fashioned ; he believed in God.' That set me thinking. I thought to myself, How much better it would be for the world if more people believed in God. I got so far as to acknowledge that for myself, if I were not to be disloyal to conscience, it was essential for me to believe in God.''

Thus matters stood with him when he was invited to the house-party at Cambridge of which mention has been made in the chapter called " A Rugger Blue." Desire to see more of F. B., a feeling in his own mind that something more was yet demanded of him than an intellectual acknowledgment of the ethical value of Christianity, made him accept this invitation.

He says that he learned during those wonderful days in Cambridge the way of believing in God. The word *spiritual* as applied to a human being, he came to see, implied a person through whom the divine spirit could work. He began from that point to understand what he calls " the intimate working of the philosophy of Jesus." Before he could reasonably hope to be in some communion with the divine spirit, manifestly he must attune his moral being to that celestial tone. His particular need, he felt, was for honesty, first with himself and then with others ; a genuine willingness to share burdens and difficulties ; a disposition to pray readily and continually, out of a sense of great need and inexpressible unworthiness ; an increasing consideration for the feelings of other people, taking into account their desires, their needs, and their limitations ; finally, a complete submission of himself to the supreme ideal of human life, Christ Jesus, with an instant and rejoicing readiness to make any sacrifice of himself and his fortunes at the call of the least of those whom he could help.

There came a moment at that house-party when he made this submission of his will to the Will of God, when he decided that henceforth he would live in absolute singleness of mind, with no thought of self, with everything he had or possessed at the service of his Master, his soul hungering and thirsting for the perfection of God.

In one of his letters to me, written before an even greater experience of spiritual power, he said : " There is much more I might say, but this will be enough just now. At every point we are called upon for sober thinking, and for discipline and for earnestness. The further I go the more profoundly am I impressed with the significance of *simplicity*. All the greatest ideas and truths in the world are simple. The Bible is simple. The highest prayer one can make or know of is the simplest of all. The issues of morality are simple—purity, honesty, sincerity, discipline. Jesus led a simple life in a humble station. The argument *ex contrarie* (i.e. that that which is not simple is probably unsound) applies forcibly to ever so many things, e.g. philosophy, if not to everything. Comparisons are odious, but we learn in time to rely on some ultimate criterion."

Since those words were written he has paid a visit to the United States in company with F. B., and from F. B. and others I learn that he has exercised a very powerful influence among American undergraduates. I do not wonder, for he is a singularly taking person. Moreover, his spiritual growth is visible to the eyes of all his friends. One of them described to me that growth as " tremendous," adding that Beau Ideal had gone in for " a most severe self-discipline," that he had " absolutely given up no end of things," that he was now " completely in the saddle," and that he allows " nothing to stand in the way of helping other men." All this I can well believe. The fire was there from the first. Such men, however long they may hold back from the dreadful moment of an absolute decision, will go to the uttermost extreme of self-sacrifice when once they have escaped from the former things of their tyranny.

It may be interesting to glance for a moment at the intellectual characteristics of his faith. He finds no difficulty in thinking of Jesus as " the propitiation for the sins of the whole world." He finds the greatest help in thinking of Jesus as the one power by whom men come to God and as the one being before whom we could not do a shameful act. He is convinced that the Bible and prayer are essential to spiritual life. In his last letter written from America he tells me that he is entering with others into " A First Century Christian Fellowship," explaining that they wish to get back to the type of Christianity which was maintained by the apostles— " We not only accept their beliefs, but are also decided to practice their methods."

He announces in detail the elemental beliefs of a First Century Christianity. He believes in :

> The possibility of immediate and continued fellowship with the Holy Spirit—*guidance.*
>
> The proclamation of a redemptive gospel—*personal, social, and national salvation.*
>
> The possession of fulness of life—*rebirth, and an ever-increasing power and wisdom.*
>
> The propagation of their life by individuals to individuals—*personal religion.*

Out of these beliefs proceeds the method of propagation :

> Love for the sinner.
> Hatred of the sin.
> Fearless dealing with sin.
> The presentation of Christ as the cure for sin.
> The sharing and giving of self, with and for others.

" We are more concerned," he writes, " with testifying to real experiences, explicable only on the hypothesis that God's power has brought them to pass, through Christ, than with teaching an abstract ethical doctrine."

From this it will be seen that there is a tendency in his mind not only to make large assumptions (that is characteristic of all practical people), but also perhaps to regard obstinate credulity as a virtue. He seems ready to take over from one particular version of the First Century any phrase or idea which that version associates with the apostles—not to take it over as poetry, or as an attempt of the Eastern mind to utter inexpressible mystery in the language of metaphor, but as an axiom in a mathematical system of thought.

I remember that in one of his former letters, speaking of the commending simplicity of the Christian religion, he remarks that the question of Jesus, *What think ye of Christ?* is simplicity itself. One is obliged to say that it is quite impossible for a man who has made even a cursory study of the documents to believe that Jesus ever asked such a question ; certainly it was never asked in that form. The word Christ was not known to Jesus, and was never applied by the Greeks to any human being until after His death. Again, it is a solitary question, remote from the whole character of the life of Jesus ; a life, we may surely say, which never wasted a moment in metaphysical speculation. Not what a man thought about Him was the preoccupation of Jesus, but whether that man was doing the Will of God. " Suffer little children to come unto Me, and forbid them not ; for of such is the Kingdom of Heaven."

The danger of enthusiasm in religion is a very definite record of history ; but if we go more deeply into that matter we shall surely find that this danger was only great and perilous to the progress of civilisation when it took the form of enthusiasm for a particular answer to the question, *What think ye of Christ ?*

Enthusiasm for love, modesty, unselfish service, moral discipline, and spiritual excellence, and the character of Jesus, has contributed to the progress of civilisation nothing but good. A movement of personal religion in our own time may render priceless service to that difficult progress, and to all the most enduring of human interests ; but one must doubt whether such a movement can ever emerge into the main current of existence if its little streams are dammed by theological tests.

I feel about Beau Ideal and those with whom he now appears to be associating himself that in their enthusiasm for the liberation and power of spiritual life they are somewhat dangerously disposed to regard theological objections to the Catholic religion as sins against the Holy Spirit, and to confuse an unquestioning credulity with the beautiful and ineffable virtue of aspiring faith.

It is natural, of course, for an impetuous and grateful mind, which has suffered sharply in the furnace of temptation, to regard with immeasurable gratitude the person who has opened to it the door of escape ; but upon each of us, surely, is laid the obligation most seriously to ask himself whether one can ever be morally justified in taking over from another man, merely because he has helped us, a dogmatic theology (which we propose henceforth to make a religious test for those we would attempt to help) without a personal and very conscientious scrutiny.

CHAPTER VII

THIS narrative illustrates one of those curious paradoxes which sooner or later confront every historian of religion who attempts to lay down hard and fast rules of spiritual experience. It is the story of a changed life with no red-letter day in its calendar. One finds no moment in its progress where a definite break was made consciously with the past. It tells of no crisis of emotion setting a term to illusion and opening the gates to illumination. It is as true a document of conversion as any to be found in the pages of *The Varieties of Religious Experience*, and yet it seems to question the familiar saying of William James that " the crisis of self-surrender has always been, and must always be, regarded as the vital turning-point of the religious life."

Perhaps such a story may be helpful and encouraging to those who have grown in spiritual happiness just as they have grown in intellectual happiness ; it will not, I hope, minister in any way to the moral indecision of those who, needing it so conspicuously, shrink from the apparent ordeal of self-surrender. For the majority of men, one suspects, the crisis is essential.

Until he was twenty years of age this agreeable American, who is now only twenty-five, made no acquaintance with dogmatic theology. He grew up in a home which took religion for granted. His father, a man of wealth, was firmly religious in the moral sense of that word ; a lawyer, and a prominent citizen of his state, he stood for " clean politics," for honest dealing in trade, and for the domestic virtues in family life. Both from this father and from his mother, who was also strongly religious in an ethical manner, the boy learned to regard a lie as cowardly and shameful, and to feel that there was something superior and honourable in straight-forwardness. The other member of the family was a sister, a little older than himself, very charming and sympathetic, of a natural refinement, and with an inclination to the deeper things of religious life.

The family was exclusive to an extreme degree. This exclusiveness was not dictated by social considerations, but by a love of privacy and quiet. The father was a cultivated man with a fine library. He loved reading, and found his chief intellectual happiness in history and biography. He encouraged his son to read the best order of books. " Never read trash," was one of his constant injunctions. He conveyed the impression that the mind could be soiled by contact with the second-rate.

There was no feeling for art in the family. Music had no place in it ; painting awoke no interest. The happiness of the household was complete, and felt no need for these things. Discussion never occurred at the table. The mind of the family was agreed upon everything. Occasionally the father would speak with contempt of a shady politician, or express himself strongly on the behaviour of a statesman or a newspaper ; but there was never anything in the nature of debate or discussion.

The son was sent to a Quaker school because it was the best in the town. Perhaps he acquired at that school something of the Quaker spirit. One sees in his handsome face a certain austerity of the spirit, and feels in his manner an almost preternatural gravity of mind. He is extraordinarily self-possessed, but without the least trace—on the contrary, indeed—of self-satisfaction or loudness of mind. The voice is low, the dark eyes are solemn, the expression of the face is impassive. He makes much the same impression on one, even in full daylight, as is made by a stranger speaking from the shadows of a large and curtained room which is lighted by a sleeping fire. It is as if he dwells far back in the recesses of his mind, so far back, at any rate, that the world can never steal his quiet or soil his peace.

At seventeen years of age he proceeded to Princeton University. There was no shock of any kind in this first acquaintance with the world. He was happy in making a friend of Richard Cleveland, son of President Cleveland, for this Richard was a social reformer very unlikely to get into wrong sets. The two young men regarded one aspect of Varsity life with great contempt. There are no colleges in Princeton ; only dormitories. In order to get something of the feeling of college life, the undergraduates form clubs, chiefly for eating purposes, and these clubs divide themselves into clubs with luxurious buildings, suitable for the rich and the distinguished, and hugger-mugger clubs, suitable for the poor student. Richard Cleveland and the man of whom I am writing regarded this state of things as vulgar and bad. Such a division, they said, set up false standards. The business of a University is to mix all sorts and conditions of men together ; to unify, not to divide ; certainly not to exalt wealth as something higher than genius or poverty. Moreover, a certain amount of drinking and gambling went on in the luxurious clubs ; the moral influence was decidedly not good. On one mind on this subject, and being prominent men in that year, they opposed themselves to the tradition. Out of a class of three hundred, they enlisted a hundred men who pledged themselves not to join the expensive and aristocratic clubs.

It must not be thought that this social activity created in the mind of our austere undergraduate a desire for public life. It is important to know that he remained aloof from personal friendships, and was intimate with no one. His influence was felt in the University with no exertion on his part. He found himself elected to offices he had never sought ; before he quite realised what had happened he discovered himself in a position of some moral responsibility. Still, he remained the quiet, serious, self contained, and reserved student, making no friends, seeking no acquaintances, inviting no confidences.

Ec

On his vacations he listened to his sister's account of religious activity at the college in which she was distinguishing herself. He was interested, felt that it was the right thing for her to be interested in such work, but there the matter ended.

When he returned to Princeton, he found himself directing a movement half social and half religious—a movement to get University men interested in boys' clubs and summer camps. At one of these summer camps he made the acquaintance of a bright and intelligent newsboy, who began to talk to him more and more seriously about religion, until one day he suddenly blurted out a confession and asked his rich young friend for advice. The undergraduate recommended cold baths, no lounging about, brisk habits of mind and body. Some months afterwards the boy drew him on one side, and said that this plan did not work, asking if there was nothing else to be tried.

The fact that he really had nothing else to advise rather preyed on the undergraduate's mind. He began to pay some attention to the question of personal religion. He heard about the work which F. B. was doing in some of the Universities. Then he met F. B. and was invited to attend a little Retreat of men interested in personal religion. He was disappointed at first in F. B. A temperamental reticence held him back for some time from joining this Retreat. But in the end he was persuaded to go, and he went with a thoroughly uncomfortable feeling, convinced that he would be a fish out of water.

He said to me, " I have never had any moral
struggle. I have never been aware of any problems
in myself. I could always get along without outside
help. Religion only interested me when I came to
see how badly other men needed it to save themselves from going on the rocks. I learned as I went
along that there are such things as temptations.
Happily for me, I was altogether unaware of such
temptations ; my tastes, my temperament, my
home-life, made certain things ugly and dislikeable
to me; but other men, I discovered, did not see those
things in the same light. Among the men who went
to F. B.'s Retreat were some whom I knew fairly
well, and knew to be doing no good. I saw these
men changed. It was the sudden and complete
change in these men, under F. B.'s influence, which
made an effect upon my mind. It was impossible
not to be impressed. I never tackled anyone myself
and nobody tackled me ; but I saw something of this
tackling, and I saw quite clearly its extraordinary
effect. Still I felt reluctant to take up any work
of that nature. It was good for other men, but
not for me. I had no bias that way, no gift for
such work. My whole temperament was opposed
to it."

Soon after this a youngish man came to the
University as Secretary of the Christian Association.
He had been changed by F. B. He talked to my
friend, told him that he too had been just as repelled
by F. B., and then proceeded to relate what F. B.
had done for him. The happiness of this man, the
tremendous drive of his personality, his reality, his
conviction that men could be saved from sin by no

other method, made a marked impression on my friend's mind.

Still, no decision was taken.

A little later there were religious conferences. F. B.'s spirit, he says, had prepared their atmosphere. It was a friendly, hopeful, and perfectly natural atmosphere. The absence of anything official or sacerdotal struck him agreeably. Men of all sorts were there—scholars and athletes—and all of them talked in their natural voices, wore ordinary clothes, and behaved as if they were debating a political question. He found himself growing more and more convinced that F. B. was right. He had no personal interview. He was simply one of a group. F. B.'s remarks were made to the whole group, never to him in particular. But gradually, profoundly, imperceptibly, the change was taking place. Day by day he became more certain. Day by day he saw what he was going to do. There was no crisis ; no moment in which he decided ; no moment in which religion suddenly became real. Everything in the old life shaded off into the new life forming within him. God did not suddenly cease to be a name and suddenly become a Person. It was all like the coming of a dawn—a gradual emergence from darkness to twilight, from twilight to day.

But the daylight was there, and he saw visibly what was before him. An only son, very expensively educated, who goes to a proud father and announces that he wishes to devote his life to the poverty and service of religion cannot be sure of congratulation. But this announcement had to be made. So great now was the gradual and

imperceptible change in his soul that he could con-
template no other life. To give all he possessed
to the work of helping men was now his destiny.

" There was no real opposition in my family," he
told me. " My sister was back in the home, engaged in religious work, and the atmosphere was
perhaps changed by her work. In any case, my
father was extremely kind and understanding. My
mother expressed a strong feeling that the step I
contemplated might not be wise, but she was quite
affectionate. Everything seemed to be made easy
for me. I took up the work, and I am happier than
I have ever been before. It has opened to me a door
to one of the greatest things in life—friendship."

He spoke of this great thing with his usual self-
mastery, and yet it was impossible not to realise an
enthusiasm in the measured words. He had no
glowing language for the mystical experiences of the
religious life, and no glowing words either for the
wonderful delight of human friendship ; but he
spoke of this high human pleasure with a certain
ring in his voice which I never caught when he was
speaking of other subjects.

He said, " I had no idea that friendship was such
a beautiful thing. I came late to it, because our
family kept so much to itself, and because by nature
I was very reserved as a boy. We never seemed to
meet other people. Certainly I never played with
other children. I met boys of my own age at school ;
but only at school ; they never came back to our
house. I never *knew* them. In a sense I had never
known anybody at all. But this work of personal
religion brings friendship into a man's life in its

highest conceivable form. I am now so rich in friends that I smile when people speak to me of the self-sacrifice in religion. The life a man lays down in this matter is not a very desirable thing. The life he takes up again is full of the deepest possible happiness. One finds that it is very difficult to help another man until one really cares for him, and directly one cares for another man not only is it easy to help him, but you get this most beautiful thing of friendship—friendship that counts no cost in its longing to be of service. I doubt if many people who live entirely without religion have any idea of what friendship is—true human friendship."

He makes one think of Bacon's great saying, " no man that imparteth his joys to his friend, but he joyeth the more ; and no man that imparteth his griefs to his friend, but he grieveth the less."

This work has not only brought him a pleasure of which he had no experience, but a new knowledge of which he had never dreamed.

" I am astounded," he said to me, " by the moral chaos in men's lives. Difficulties about which I knew nothing present themselves now at every turn. Sin, I discover, plays an unimaginably great part in human life. Men who might be of service to a nation, and who might enjoy peace of mind and a life of the highest happiness, are frustrated by inclinations which they find themselves powerless to resist, even when they see clearly that they are disastrous. I used to think that a man went to the bad because he liked going to the bad. It always seemed to me that men who did things which most decent men regard as unworthy or even contemptible, did those things because they found pleasure in them.   Now I know that many of these men, at any rate at the beginning of their careers, do these things against their own judgment, even against their own will.   Something within them drives them on.   They are suddenly attacked by irresistible power.   They describe themselves as being forced, driven, or hurled into ways which they hate.   All this was at one time quite unintelligible to me.   I never realised that there is a struggle in the soul.   Now I know that any man whose personality is divided must always live at the sport of treacherous inclinations."

He also said to me : " I do not at all think that sex difficulties are the chief battle-ground of youth.   I regard those difficulties as much the same as lethargy, pride, idleness, coldness, meanness, selfishness.   It is even harder sometimes to break down a man's conceit or selfishness than to strengthen another man against sensual weakness.   All sin has its roots in selfishness.   Chaos is inseparable from selfishness."

He spoke to me also of his view concerning the future of religion in the struggle of man's soul.

" I have learned," he said, " from this work of personal religion to distrust organisation and to see a quite extraordinary power in the leaven of personality.   No doubt organisation of some kind will long continue, and will be useful ; but I feel confident that the future belongs to personal religion, by which I mean the unofficial, the unprofessional, and the un-institutional influence of one man on another.   I am quite sure humanity must be saved man by man, not in droves and herds. I doubt if anyone can profoundly help another until he cares for him as a friend. And until intercourse is absolutely intimate how can one soul understand another soul—understand it in such a manner as to render help ? "

He told me of the change which is now going on in the Universities of America. There is a new seriousness among undergraduates, an increasing sense of responsibility, a visible movement towards spiritual life. All this is entirely due to personal religion. It is the work of a few men like F. B. It has received no impetus from official quarters. Swiftly, as if some mysterious power were at work, the spirit spreads from University to University, and religion becomes a real thing, a thing of infinite moment to the individual, of enormous importance to the future of the human race.

Directly, he says, a man feels that religion is a real power in human life, not merely a subject for theological discussion, he becomes interested in it. And directly he discovers that it can work a miracle in his own soul he seeks to understand it. A few men with this wonderful leaven of personality could change the world.

CHAPTER VIII

A YOUNG SOLDIER

ONE of the guests at the house-party to which I referred in my introduction was pointed out to me as a man who had distinguished himself in the war by notable courage. He looked a mere boy— one of those fresh-skinned, fair-haired, urchin-like striplings whose faces flush with a grinning self-consciousness when they find themselves objects of observation.

He was tall and slight, with an inclination to stoop his head. But for the sadness of his voice, which is rather deep in note, and the gravity of his words in discussion, one would think of him as a sly schoolboy always on the alert to pull somebody's leg or to work off a pun. So much suppressed laughter, so much restrained gaiety, so much controlled roguishness, it would be difficult to find in the face of the most frivolous-minded tormentor of a schoolmaster. It was difficult for me to think of this jolly-looking youth as a soldier ; more difficult to believe that he had passed through a religious crisis.

He told me that his father, who was a well-known man in English public life, died when he was eight years of age. " Yet," he said, " my impression of him is quite clear ; his personality was unforgettable."

As for his mother, who is still alive, he declared that she is a mother beyond all praise.

In a home so enviable as this, with one brother as a companion, M. grew up to boyhood, not merely shielded from all coarse influences which might throw miserable shadows across the radiance of a child's natural innocence, but encouraged to find his highest delight in occupations wholesome both for mind and body. The books he read were calculated to develop refinement of spirit ; the games he played were calculated to develop his courage and his muscles. When he went to a preparatory school he was as good a specimen of healthy, hearty, clean-minded, and intelligent English boyhood as any father could wish to see.

Unhappily for his development, there was a master at this school who was tormented by a devil of lust, and whose evil and furtive spirit corrupted the whole school. The boy learned vice at the hands of one who was paid to teach him virtue. He appears to have slipped into bad habits, as so many small boys do, with no apprehension at all of their consequences, physical or moral. Nevertheless he was not without knowledge that what he did was wrong, that it was something to be done out of sight, that it was an act of which he felt ashamed. It was with a feeling of relief that he found himself in a public school, where the moral tone was healthier and where he came under the stimulating influences of " some ripping masters."

Dogged by the vice he had learned at his first school, M. made a gallant fight for his self-respect, and gradually obtained a fair mastery over dangerous dispositions. He did well in games and well in school. He began to enjoy himself with the happiness of one who feels that things are straightening out, that the path before him leads to success, and that success can be gained with comparative ease. He won a scholarship for Oxford, and went up to the University with an appetite for all the best things which life offers at its charming threshold to the happiest order of manhood—that order of manhood which finds as superlative a pleasure in the acquisition of knowledge as in an increasing skill in difficult games.

One term of great happiness passed away, and then came the European war, claiming him as a soldier of England. From others I learn that he rose quickly to the rank of captain, that he was distinguished throughout his service for an unquailing courage and a singularly gentle regard for the welfare of his men, and that he won enviable distinctions in the great Battle of the Somme, falling at last to an attack of poison-gas.

When he recovered from this rather desperate affliction he was sent back to Oxford. The war had weakened in him his enthusiasm for scholarship, and had heightened in him his passion for games. He found an extraordinary delight in physical fitness. As if war had whetted his appetite for danger, he loved chiefly those games which involved risk of limb. When he could not play such games he rode about the country on a motor-cycle, loving speed for itself and almost seeking those " narrow squeaks " which make the elderly spectator hold his breath.

It was in the rush of this athletic period, when his

body was at its fittest and his mind freest from anxiety, that sexual trouble began once more to invade. But Oxford provided for him at this time something of an aid in his distress. He discovered the pleasure of friendship. There were rooms in which he was always welcome ; there were delightful men always willing to talk. Among these men it was natural to discuss religion, and religion came back to his mind, consecrated by the memory of his father, and sacred with the thought of his mother, to help him in the loneliness of his conflict. But the stir of sex in his blood was not to be stilled, and though he might again and again overthrow that powerful motion in his whole being, yet the thing was there, haunting him, irking him, gnawing at his self-respect, shadowing his natural happiness.

In one of his discussions with a friend he heard for the first time of F. B., and was curious rather than interested by what he heard. At any rate he made no effort to see F. B., and continued to fight his battle in his own way. Soon after this he was badly broken in a Rugger smash, and was carted off to hospital with more injuries to his bones than the Great War had been able to inflict.

One day, lying in his bed at this hospital, a stranger came to see him. It was F. B. F. B. had been told by one of M.'s friends that there was a man in hospital who might be glad, he rather thought, to have a talk with him. Accordingly F. B., brisk, smiling, and quietly cheerful, presented himself at the bedside of football's victim.

" He made no impression upon me," said M., " neither one way nor the other. It never occurred

to me to think of him as an out-of-the-way sort of
person. He seemed perfectly natural, not particularly interesting, and certainly not in the least
striking. But after he had left me I was conscious of
a very curious feeling about him. I wanted to see
him again. It wasn't a case of wanting to see a
person one likes, or a person who has interested one
by his ideas, but wanting to see a man who had made
no other impression except this curious and inexplicable impression that one did very much want to see
him again."

The next time F. B. came to M.'s bedside he made
another impression. He was still an average person,
still a person who was not in the least dramatic or
even notable, yet he left behind him in M.'s mind the
distinct sensation that he could help him. " I
couldn't explain to myself why I had this feeling,"
M. told me ; " I tried to reason the thing out, but
couldn't see the ghost of an explanation. We had
said nothing of a serious nature. There was no sense
of intimacy. I was still conscious of his difference as
a Yankee. And yet there it was ; I could not shake
out of my mind the notion that this unremarkable
man could help me to straighten things out as no
other man had yet done."

F. B.'s account of the matter is as follows : " One
of his friends had spoken to me about him. He
mentioned no trouble, but said that M. was a man
he'd like me to meet. He spoke of his services in the
war, told me about his fame as a Rugger player, said
he was altogether a very fine fellow, and then
mentioned that he was lying in the hospital, cracked

up pretty badly. I knew I had to see this man. I knew, too, directly I saw him what his trouble was. We talked of just ordinary things. I didn't bother to know whether he liked me or not ; all I knew was that for certain he would one day ask me to help him.

"That day came. He didn't find it easy to tell me the whole story. He got as far, with great difficulty, as telling me that he wasn't as happy as he wanted to be, and that he thought I might possibly be able to help him. I helped him right there, at that very moment. I helped him by telling him what his trouble was. It hit him like a blow from a hammer. After that it was easy for him, easy for me, easy for God. He's one of the finest fellows living, brave as a lion, yet shy as a girl. A beautiful nature—a real man with all the delicacy of a woman.

"Directly the trouble was out in the open he really hated it. With this hatred was a longing for all that a good man means by the Name of God. There was no wrestle, no struggle. He came to himself in a moment. Already he has done remarkable work, and when he has taken his degree as a doctor he will use his life entirely for God."

M. tells me that one of the greatest things F. B. did for him was freeing his mind for discussing this moral trouble with other men. An enormous change came into his life directly the sense of secret shame was dissipated. The evil lost its power. He found himself possessed of an altogether new strength. He was conscious of an altogether new liberty.

To complete the happiness of his freedom from a noxious obsession he found that he could help other men to get their various temptations into the open, and that once in the open it was easy for them—most of them, at any rate—to realise the need for hating their sins before they could expect answers to their prayers.

I asked him to tell me what his opinion was of the morals of men at the Universities. He replied that, so far as his experience went, the present generation of young men is a healthy one. There is no " smuttiness " among them. The vast majority want to conquer their bad habits. It would be a very gross perversion of the truth to think of these young men as accepting vice as the natural order of things. They don't narrate their adventures. They don't compare their experiences. They don't talk about these matters ; certainly those who do don't talk flippantly. There is a terrible struggle going on. It is a silent struggle. There are many defeats in that struggle, but no surrender on the part of the average man. Sport helps them more than orthodox religion, for orthodox religion seems to ignore this tremendous battlefield of youth ; at any rate, it has nothing to offer which is recognised by the fighters as a help. What does help, what does enable most men to get the victory, is the personal religion inculcated by F. B. And there is far more of this work going on than the dons know. It is a part of a friendship of University life, widening its influence with every term.

One of the stories he told me, very modestly, of his own efforts to help other men is well worth telling here. In none of these stories (need I assert it of so

gallant and gentle a man?) was there the least
suggestion of exalting his own power over other lives.
His sole object in telling them was to show me how
the drive of sympathy can help a man who rather
shrinks from such work to change the lives of others.
His great contention is that F. B. has discovered for
him the central truth of spiritual life, the pearl of
great price, and that this truth is destined to save
the soul of the world. He is quite sure about that.
The soul can definitely deal direct with God.

Among his fellow medical students he came across
a man who had been with him at his public school.
They renewed the friendship of those days, found
that they had been fighting together in France
without knowing it, and gradually entered into an
intimate relationship.

This friend of schooldays told M. that when he
went out to France he was engaged to be married.
The brutality of the war atmosphere, with its
manifold depressions and its inescapable temptations, preyed upon his moral energy, chafing him,
but could not impair his loyalty to the girl in
England. For two years of constant danger and
surrounding bestiality he kept faith with idealism.
He was as true as steel. Then he returned from the
war to find that this girl had formed another attach-
ment and wished to throw him over.

In the bitterness of his grief and the irony of his
disillusion he went to the dogs. Alone in London,
hating his solitude, longing for sympathy, and
tortured by the thought that he had been true to a
woman in vain, he sought to forget his troubles in
the society of harlots. Revulsion overcame him after

every one of these visits, a revulsion bitter as gall, but again and again he went back, driven by an intolerable sense of loneliness. "Many men," he told M., "go to these poor girls simply for companionship. They are the kindest people in London to the friendless man eating his heart out in lodgings."

The manner in which M. has been able to help this particular person is simply by giving him a sense of loyalty to his own higher nature and by providing him with an altogether more abiding companionship. But the bitterness of the man's heart is not yet wholly gone, and the sense of the divine companionship is not yet firmly established. Still is he overtaken from time to time by an unbearable feeling of solitude and forlornness ; but now, instead of seeking a cure for that ill where no cure is to be found, he comes to M., and to M. confesses his feebleness. "We are helping each other," is M.'s account of the matter.

No man could be freer than M. from that insufferable arrogance, or self-satisfaction, which disfigures so many people who feel themselves to be called by God to the service of converting other men. He speaks with quiet reverence, but an extreme diffidence, of his belief that his power to help other men is increasing, and he looks forward to the day when as a doctor in some foreign Christian mission he may be able to exert that power with far greater effect. The power is there. He has no doubt about that. The ability to use it must be determined by his own response to its unaltering conditions.

He seems to me to be studying the laws of the

spiritual world as the man of science studies the law
of the physical world. He is rightly making experi-
ments with his soul. But below the inquiring mind is
a spirit which believes unquestionably and with deep
gladness in the existence of a God who is desirous
of communicating Himself to His creature ; and in
the mind itself, that mind which inquires and investi-
gates, is the clear knowledge that hatred of sin, and a
clean bill from all forms of selfishness, must go before
that craving desire for moral wisdom which estab-
lishes connection with the Eternal Righteousness.
He does not announce himself as a discoverer, but
he is certainly a traveller.

The moral and spiritual difference separating such
men as this charming young person from the offensive
type of evangelical who went about in the eighties
asking everyone whom he encountered, " Are you
saved ? " seem to me as great as the moral and
spiritual differences which separate the writings of
Plato from the writings of Ibsen, or the life of John
Hampden from the life of Rousseau. It is an entirely
new type. It is a phenomenon in religious experience. With all the earnestness and unflinching
realism of the older type of evangelicalism there is a
delicacy, a modesty, a sweetness, and a tolerance
in this new protagonist of personal religion which
renders him, I think, a force of great hope for the
future.

CHAPTER IX

THE VIRGINIAN

HERE, to wind up these brief narratives, is the story of a blithe and hard-hitting spirit whose blood may well have descended to him from those Englishmen, " the flower and force of a kingdom," as Sir John Smyth described them to Lord Burghley in the sixteenth century, who then fought in Flanders and who " went voluntary to serve of a gaiety and joyalty of mind."

The vigour of the man, the sheer delight he gets out of his struggle, the uncompromising character of his attack, and the warm friendliness of his nature, should bring him close enough to the people in England who still acknowledge the ancient tradition of Elizabethan adventure. The phrase used of F. W. Robertson may well be used of him. He is a *troubadour of God.*

He was born in a fox-hunting country, beautiful with the softness and tenderness of our English shires, with far views from the hilltops over Chesapeake Bay to the rim of the Atlantic. His father owned a considerable estate, and the boy grew up among many negro servants, innumerable animals, and a regular Zoo of pets. There was a certain sense of lordship in his mind. He liked his own way, felt himself irritated by check, stung by correction, and incapable of seeing life from any point of view but his own.

During his boyhood the central figure of the family life was a venerable snow-capped grandmother, more Victorian than Victoria herself, mildly morbid about a long-deceased husband, evangelical, rigid concerning the proprieties, her austere and commanding face sternly set against invading vulgarity, but copious and anecdotal, with an interest in the living world, albeit an interest chiefly anxious concerning its future.

Under the shadow of this impressive relic of a vanished antiquity the soul of the mutinous boy was chilled into some semblance of reverence, coming from his ponies and dogs into her presence with the sense of entering another world, breathing a different climate, speaking an unnatural language.

It was only when he was alone with his mother that he felt stirrings within him of tenderness and graciousness. He told me that she was "always interested in what I was doing, but never solicitous "—a telling phrase good for all mothers to lodge in their hearts. His mother never gave him the feeling that he was being watched ; he could talk to her without the paralysing fear that she was listening only in order to correct ; a beautiful frankness, a real interest in his affairs, a quick willingness to help him on his own level, characterised her attitude ; and when he wished to be alone she understood and withdrew to other occupations.

From this mother he learned to think of a transcendent Being who had created the heavens and the earth, and of His Son Jesus, who had lived among men, who had taught them how to live, and who had been cruelly put to death by wicked enemies.

This teaching was associated in his mind with the different activities which marked one day in the week, when he had to be more careful in his use of soap and flannel, when his best suit was put out for him, and when he went in company with his parents to a church carrying on the Anglican tradition. There, too, he found the secular importance of his father duly acknowledged, for his father was one of the " patrons " of that church, and was ever received with a certain deference by the other officials.

What the boy thought of God and Christ, of Heaven and Hell, of Prayers and Hymns, we do not know ; for his consciousness did not become alert in such matters till he was approaching the age of fourteen. It woke suddenly to awareness, and also to enthusiasm, in rather a strange way. There came to that church one Sunday a very old clergyman who had spent long years of his life as a missionary to the mountaineers in the Far South. Such stories did he tell in his sermon, stories of pathos and heroism, stories of difficulties and endurance, stories of violent men broken down by the beauty of Christ, and bad men restored to goodness and happiness by the power of Christ, that the little boy in the big pew resolved then and there that he too would be a missionary.

The strange feature in this idea is its tenacity. It did not fly in at one door of his soul and out at the other, like Bede's sparrow ; it stayed there, worked

there, became the master-thought of his mind
When he was in the fields, or among his animals, or
talking to the negroes, this idea went to sleep ; but
when he came to lie down in his bed at night it
awoke with a freshness that held his thoughts. He
began to read the Bible with a boy's earnest atten-
tiveness, to say his prayers with no mere formal sense
of fulfilling a duty, to cultivate an interest in the
history of the Church. Nevertheless, he still
remained the proud and self-willed little boy of the
years before this dream.

Soon after the visit of the missionary he was
packed off to a "Church School," which is an
American equivalent for the English public school,
and his clerical ambition was not daunted by the
visible and even scandalous enmity which existed
between the clergymen who taught him his lessons,
preached to him in church about the gospel, and
administered to him the sacrament of Holy Communion. These men disliked each other quite openly,
and did not hide that ugly fact, in which they
gloried, from the boys under their care.

He says that the religious studies of this school
were "lifeless, sapless," but gladly acknowledges
that the tone was good, and says that his spiritual
life was helped in the fields and by the sea. There
was not a boy in the school who had come from a
bad home.

From this school he proceeded to one of the best
Universities of America, and soon became a figure in
its most fashionable club (a form of college), ending
up as a member of its Senior Council, and the
President of the undergraduate religious Society in

the University.   He was of a nature to make an impression.

The war in Europe brought him in 1915 to the British Islands with a group of American University men who had volunteered to serve with the Y.M.C.A. He worked like a nigger, but confesses that if he touched one man that summer it was all he did, and that man not vitally.

His next spiritual adventure was in China, where his University maintains an important college.   He says he was astonished by the wonderful machine he found in China, but more astonished by the fact that it did nothing—" machinery, but no motion."   He was told by all the workers that he was doing wonderful things, but he knew very well that he was doing nothing.   The business school, the gymnasium, the library, the classes, the social work—all these were crowded by young Chinamen ; but what came of them ?   When Ruskin was told that a submarine cable had been laid between England and India he asked, " What messages will it convey ? "

One day there came to this Chinese city the Surgeon of Souls, with a group of men devoted to the work of personal religion.   He was pointed out to the Virginian in this fashion : " There goes a man who is doing what these missionaries and Christian workers are talking about."   The Virginian took a good look at him and did not like him.   He thought him crude. The attitude of the aristocratic University towards the college where F. B. had begun to work was one of supercilious contempt.   The Virginian shared that contempt.

But interest in F. B. increased, and the Virginian

found himself listening to stories about him. Presently he was making F. B.'s acquaintance, and found him, rather condescendingly perhaps, a person worth knowing. One day he drew F. B. aside and asked him if he would tackle a certain young Chinaman in whom he was interested. F. B. replied, " That's your job. If you haven't anything to give him by now you ought to ! " The Virginian was mad. He went away, not sorrowfully, but in a towering rage.

When this temper evaporated he faced the truth of F. B.'s bitter taunt. Nothing to give ! Was that really the truth ? If so, how serious, how impossible, his position. He fought with himself. Was he to give up his hope of helping men ? Would it always be that he had nothing to give ? The question drove him to F. B.

" One day," he tells me, " we got to business. I told him, in spite of myself, my temptations and my sins. They came out almost before I knew it. For the first time they were outside myself, in words, words that startled and shamed. He understood. We got it all into the open. The position became absolutely clear. I saw at once what was keeping me from power. There was no overflow, because there was no inflow, and no inflow because sin was walling out the power of God. I tried to bring up intellectual difficulties. He refused to discuss them, would not even glance at them. This may seem to some—it didn't to me—a source of weakness ; it gives the impression that he cares nothing for intellectual integrity. The truth is the man is a born mystic. Get him alone and you realise this at once. And you realise also the truth of what William James says, that we have got to accept the experience of the mystic as valid experience. F. B. made a tremendous impression on me. His simple insistence on the power of sin to wall out any vital consciousness of God was irresistible. He showed me, quite mercilessly, my spiritual impotence in the lives of other men. He laid it all bare to me, naked in broad daylight, my spiritual impotence. What good was I ? Let a man ask himself that question. It's a searcher."

That night the Virginian tried to pray, but felt that his prayer was useless. He knew that he was at a turning-point. Either he would go back to America and surrender to the world, or—— The point that frightened him was this : If he took the plunge it might mean, not a decorative interest in religion, not the patronising association of a rich young man with a University scheme of social welfare, but the mission-field for life. Was he ready for that ? To be a parson ?

He walked about his room. " My sins," he said, " rose up before me straight as tombstones. If I took this plunge it meant a clearing up all along the line. It meant confession. It meant a break with all that had gone before—a new life. Then I saw that this was a matter of the will, not of the intellect. I faced that knowledge for several moments. My will ! Was I willing to do this thing, or was I not willing ? A strange thought, annihilating in its effect—my little pygmy will opposed to the Will of God, my little pride sniffing at the Universe, my heart dead cold in the Presence of the Almighty !

Without a scrap of emotion, but with what I can only call a great heave of my will, I knelt down to make my submission, to give myself, without reservation, to God. Usually this moment costs something in nervous energy, and results in emotional excitation. I experienced nothing of the kind. I was sensible only of calm, of a feeling that something needful and right had been done. I felt very little at the time. I simply realised that I had jumped a fence at which I had long balked. There was no breaking in of light upon me, nor anything unusual. After the prayer, which tore away a wall of my own erection—the wall of unwillingness to face God's Will fully—I prayed again, but without ecstasy. I rose from that prayer hoping that I might be used to help others, and feeling that I had done what was required of me. But I was not to be left only with that feeling. As I lay in bed there came to me a distinct Voice, and that Voice, said, *There is no work of Mine to do for him who is not wholly Mine.* I cannot tell you the effect of those words. They were no words of mine. They were different from all other words I had ever heard. And they revealed to me what I believe to be the central truth of religion."

The change in the Virginian from that hour was visible to all his friends. He became the impassioned champion of personal religion. Gone for him was all hesitancy. Abandoned, too, was the attitude of a looker-on. He flung himself with a joyful enthusiasm into the work of helping men face to face, swept forward from all his former landmarks by the immediate success of his efforts. He told me that association with F. B. taught him "the absolute workability of the thing he talked about." This was no question, remember, of dogma or of ceremonial rite. It was the human question. It was a case of drowning men saved from death. F. B. spoke of men who were "suffering hell," or of men lost in a fog, or of men who were missing all the things that make life splendid, and showed him those same men with shining eyes, glad voices, happy as the day is long. There they were before the Virginian's eyes— miracles. Changed men ! A wonderful thought ; changed from darkness to light, from blindness to vision, from misery to happiness, from death to life, laughing in the joy of that change.

What a power, to do these things !

He exclaimed to me, " I hear people say that what men want is *something quite human*. Nonsense ! What they want is something wholly and absolutely divine. The mistake lies in expressing this Divine Something in dark and mysterious language. The language must be human. But the thing itself, the mysterious Power which changes life in a moment, *that* must be shown from the first as divine. I see it in this manner : In each one of us there is a capacity for the Christ. It is the light that lighteth every man. Until sin has blotted out from consciousness the knowledge of this light, every man feels that there is something within him higher than himself I am certain this feeling exists in all men who are not dead in sin—the greatest of men of science and the most ragged and ignorant of down-and-outers. It is there in their souls, making for a sense of dualism, dividing their personality, distracting their unity. And I am equally convinced that when a man is acutely conscious of this division, and meditates on the best way of securing inward peace, he naturally, instinctively, inevitably turns to Christ. This is my firm conviction. It is born of experience. The surrender, if it is to be made, is to Christ, to no one else. To Christ, the lover and saviour of men. This is my theology : God has left a part of Himself in each of us, and this divine part of our nature, in every moral crisis, recognises the historic Jesus and the Christ of experience as its necessary complement. Of course, the traditional, the ecclesiastical, the theological mind has obscured Him ; but I am certain that where men are unprejudiced, where they are in dead earnest about getting right, where they want unity with the whole heart, the whole spirit, and the whole mind, they turn to Christ. Let me sum it all up in a few words. What changes life is, first, a sense of sin, a haunting knowledge that the habits of sin have got one in their deadly grip, second, an experience of the *hilarity* of Christianity really lived, and, third, the immense appeal of Christ's challenge to make a new world."

On no other subject is this fighting Virginian so glad to talk as the hilarity of the religious life. " The gayest bunch of men I know," he tells you, " is the group that swings round F. B. They are fellows who have found something worth finding. We never meet but what we have a good time. This is far from the professional mirth of certain sorts of religious people. It is the laughter of men who really know there is a way out in this world, and who are doing their best to make it known to others."

No defence for such happiness is necessary. It is a happiness that cannot be helped. Do men gather thorns of vines or thistles of fig-trees ? As the sun shines so does the heart of a man conscious of unity with his Creator, conscious, too, of power to change human life, rejoice with a joy unknown to the victims of delusion and the slaves of sin.

In this hilarity one sees the joy of a spirit set free from the contagion of the world's slow stain, emancipated from all the petty conventions and parochial restraints of that old, unhappy world, launched definitely on the radiant ocean of eternity. The world looks upon these men as " odd," but it has no idea how odd it looks to them. What a dull world, what a sad world, what a blind world, and what a stupid, blundering world it must seem, in the eyes of men whose hearts know nothing except the bliss of conscious and unselfish union with God. The Virginian's favourite saying of Christ is the challenge, " My doctrine is not Mine, but His that sent Me. If any man will do His will, he shall know of the doctrine, whether it be of God, or whether I speak of Myself." He says that those who have experienced this mighty change do not speak of what they think or of what they hope, but of what they *know* That is the reward of a unified personality.

Even after that night when he made his submission the Virginian has grown in this knowledge. He tells me that F. B. asked him in those early days to attend a private conference on the subject of personal religion, promising him that he should meet

a wonderful group of men—" All F. B.'s geese are
swans ; it is partly his intense enthusiasm and belief
in us which keeps us functioning ! " When he got
to his conference the Virginian was disappointed by
what looked like a lot of quite ordinary folks. The
wall arose once more between him and the souls of
others. F. B., reading his thoughts, drew him aside,
and whispered into his ear this question, " What
would you have thought of the twelve apostles ? "

From that moment he learned not only to abandon
a superior attitude towards others, and not only to
suspect and examine the grounds of instinctive antipathy, but positively to look always for the good in
others, to stand tiptoe to welcome the spiritual truth
behind all physical appearances, to become a realist
of human existence. The last vesture of self was
torn away. He became a troubadour of God.

> I profess no other share,
> In the selection of my lot, than this
> My ready answer to the will of God
> Who summons me to be His organ. All
> Whose innate strength supports them shall succeed
> No better than the sages.

He might so easily have been a conventional figure
in American life, of no more use to the universe than
a mushroom, a dull, unimaginative, and self-satisfied
citizen of a materialistic civilisation. Most of us say
at one time or another :

> The world is too much with us ; late and soon,
> Getting and spending we lay waste our powers ;
> Little we see in Nature that is ours ;

but not many think how definitely dreary is such an existence, or realise that there is a way out—a way out into unity and joy.

Let any man who reads these words ask himself whether he knows any way out of this suffocating and soul-destroying materialism save only the way taken by the Virginian—that plunge away from self, that baptism in the moving waters of God—which surely we may hope are " for ever at their priest-like task of pure ablution round earth's human shores." And the reward !

> Are there not, Festus, are there not, dear Michal,
> Two points in the adventure of a diver,
> One—when, a beggar, he prepares to plunge,
> One—when, a prince, he rises with his pearl ?
> Festus, I plunge.

" Again, the Kingdom of Heaven is like unto a merchant man, seeking goodly pearls, who, when he had found one pearl of great price, went and sold all that he had, and bought it "

During the six years which have elapsed since the first edition of this book, the work of F. B. has become known to such a world-wide extent that it is no longer possible to maintain his anonymity. The addition of the following chapter has been made necessary by the insistent demand from many sources to know more of his life and work.

THE GROUPS[1]

A Rediscovery of Spiritual Reality in Terms of Modern Life

BY JOHN MCCOOK ROOTS

" We have found all the questions that can be found.
It is time we gave up looking for questions and started
looking for answers."—G. K. CHESTERTON.

I

WHEN the Church fails, God sends a man.

Since the Middle Ages there have been three
awakenings, each about two centuries apart, each of
which forced upon a reluctant world some neglected
aspect of truth. St. Francis sought to free men from
bondage to things, Martin Luther from bondage to
institutions and dogmas, John Wesley from lethargy.

Since Wesley, nearly a century and a half has
passed. The language with which he stirred the
placid rationalism of two hundred years ago would
not arouse a flicker of interest to-day. But something is needed to do for the twentieth century what
he did for the eighteenth. It is not something
new that is needed so much as a rediscovery of the
power which lies hidden in the simplest Christian

[1] Originally printed in the *Atlantic Monthly*, December 1928.

platitudes. As Coleridge has it, " Truths, of all others the most awful and interesting, are too often considered as so true, that they lose all the power of truth, and lie bedridden in the dormitory of the soul, side by side with the most despised and exploded errors." His remedy is not easy, but it is simple : " To restore a commonplace truth to its first uncommon lustre, you need only translate it into action."

A small but growing group of people with whom I have only lately become well acquainted seem to me to be doing this. They seek to apply in their own lives the teachings of the New Testament. They work, so far as possible, within the established Churches, but they also reach, and reach effectively, people, particularly young people, who ordinarily would never darken the doors of a church. Masses mean little to them ; individuals everything. They are interested, not so much in theoretical aspects of religion or God or Christ as in the daily life which these demand. Each one is convinced, on the basis of personal experience, that God is a reality ; that the only barrier which can prevent a man from knowing God is sin, conscious or unconscious ; that Jesus Christ is the saviour from sin, and that a man is cleansed in so far as he wills to receive Him, recognising his faults as sins and turning from them to a life of unflinching devotion to the particular will of God revealed through prayer, expectant listening, and active witness with others. They hold nothing that is not taught in the Gospels and described in the Acts and Epistles. They believe nothing that Christians of all creeds do not profess to believe. Their chief difference lies in the

uncompromising manner in which they apply their
beliefs to life.

Many people to-day, whatever they profess,
assume that, for all practical purposes, Christ's
standards must be adapted to human nature. This
group act on the assumption that human nature
must be adapted to the moral standards of Jesus
Christ. They believe that human nature can be
remoulded radically toward meeting those standards.
In other words, they believe in Conversion. Many
people to-day, while professing belief in prayer and
a divine purpose, pray only in spasms, and have
never stopped long enough to consider that God
might have a purpose for them at variance with the
one they are restlessly or recklessly or hazily
pursuing. This group takes it for granted that a
converted life can be guided in all things by God's
Holy Spirit working through the human mind.
They believe that prayer, for most people who ever
pray, consists too much in petition. They too
believe in petition. But they believe first in submission and audition—surrender and listening.
They aim to shape their daily course of action on
promptings of the Holy Spirit in the form of
luminous thoughts which may come at any time,
but come most fruitfully in the quiet of the early
morning, and which can never come at all except as
their own lives are purged of self-will and remain
perpetually poised in eagerness to receive and
follow the divine direction. They are convinced
that this sort of active communion with God is
not only interesting and satisfying, but that it is
available to all. In a word, they believe in Guidance,

and this involves, not only guided work, sleep, eating, recreation, and rest, but also guided witness. Some people may find that they must talk less ; others that they should talk more ; others that they simply talk differently. But on each one who has found this quality of life is laid the obligation of conveying it to the world—a world composed, not of humanity, but of human beings. With everyone a worker in his own environment for the same end, there has been born among this group a richness of spiritual fellowship which is the rarest thing I know.

II

My junior year at Harvard, during the winter of 1923–1924, was the occasion of my first contact with it—a small cluster of college men gathered over the week-end at a wayside inn near Cambridge to talk honestly about what life had meant so far, and what it might mean. I had just come from one of the great student conventions whose business it is to discuss religion, and was in no mood for more. But the friend who asked me had said that this was a " house-party," that I should meet there an interesting person who had known my father in China, that I could say whatever I wished and leave at any time.

Two characteristics of that group particularly impressed me. One was its difference from much which I had previously associated with religion—the people were happy without being professional, the leaders were sympathetic without being solicitous, and there was no formality or programme. The other point was the transparent honesty of the atmosphere. The first quality made me feel immediately at home. The second conveyed the thought, to me a discovery, that God is real to a man only in proportion as he seeks to apply in his own life the moral standards of Jesus Christ. I had known and accepted the idea in theory. Never before had I heard any normal person of my years speak of Christ as a cure for impurity or a power for honesty. I left this house-party realising for the first time that many of my professed beliefs or unbeliefs had a moral basis, and knowing that there were abroad in the world modern people whose religion was a tempting reality.

The movement of which this was my first glimpse began, as all spiritual movements have begun, with an individual. He is F. N. D. Buchman, an ordained Lutheran minister, just turned fifty. He was born at Pennsburg, Pennsylvania—town and State both named after the founder of the Society of Friends, William Penn—and took his Bachelor's and Master's degrees from Muhlenberg College, which recently conferred upon him an honorary D.D. Naturally shy and reserved, in his student days he was hardly the sort one would have expected to recapture for the twentieth century something of the radiance of St. Francis, the mysticism of Fox, the evangelism of Wesley.

Like the founder of Methodism, he finished his seminary course still a stranger to the white heat of Christian experience. Anxious for further training, he spent a year of graduate study abroad. On his return he accepted the pastorate of a church among the working people of Philadelphia, leaving this charge at the end of three years to found the first Lutheran hospice and settlement house for poor boys. A difference with the trustees led to his resignation in protest at what he considered their insufficient provision of food for the boys, and in 1908 he again went abroad, this time expressly to attend the religious convention at Keswick, England. He was unhappy and perplexed. Resentment against certain of the trustees festered in his heart. For some time he had had an uneasy feeling that this was causing the trouble. Always pride had forbidden humiliation before these men against whom he felt he had a just grievance.

Out of this welter of internal conflict, however, conviction was gaining strength that what he lacked was a personal experience of Jesus Christ. It was not a new method that was needed, but a new man.

While in this state of mind, he wandered one day into a little country church where a woman was speaking on some aspect of the Cross. He does not know her name, but something in what she said stirred him to the depths, and he saw himself for what he truly was. It marked the turning-point. Next day he mailed to America six letters of simple apology, and at the head of each he wrote :—

" When I survey the wondrous Cross
  On which the Prince of Glory died,
My richest gain I count but loss,
  And pour contempt on all my pride."

He never heard from those six men. But for the first time in his life he felt the power of Christ as an inward reality. It was what Johann Tauler, Luther's spiritual father, used to emphasise as the " unmaking " of a man that he might be " made again " of God.

From then on his doubts left him. " Sin," he has since explained, " is anything that keeps one from God or from another person." The sin of pride had been burned away, and the explorer set out to share his discovery with others.

In 1909 he was recommended by Dr. Mott to head the Y.M.C.A. at a large State university. It was no sinecure. The students were hostile, the faculty politely sceptical. Mass evangelism obviously had no place. Personal contacts had. Religious societies in university centres are apt to count heads. The young " Y " secretary knew better. He believed now that no man was fully won to Christ until he himself was winning other men.

Three men stood out to him as key-points of the situation—the college dean, a popular and cultured graduate student, and " Bill Pickle," leading bootlegger of a ring that was the despair of the college authorities. The student, who had a fondness for codes of ethics, had styled himself a Confucianist. To his surprise, Buchman took him seriously, and banteringly suggested that if Confucianism was good for him it should be good for someone else. He dared him to try it on Mike Milligan, a chicken thief with wide reputation in the neighbourhood. By this time they were close friends, and the challenge was accepted. He was to have three months preaching Confucianism. Week after week the earnest young altruist called on the family. He was kind to the wife, gave presents to the children. But Mike remained unchanged. At the end of his period the student returned to admit defeat. " I can't do anything," he said. " The more I give the more they want." Buchman suggested they start together on Bill the bootlegger. He won the man's confidence ; and before long the worst influence in college was not only changed himself, but determined to win his fellow-professionals to Christ. The undergraduate was so struck by it all that he decided to try this religion which had succeeded where he had failed. The dean was a confirmed agnostic, but, finding his disciplinary duties lightened by improvement in the liquor situation, he was increasingly drawn to the faith that could achieve such modern miracles, and finally put himself on record as an active believer. Within three years there were twelve hundred men in voluntary Bible study.

III

Leaving this university in 1915, Buchman toured for a year in India, Korea, and Japan with Sherwood Eddy, returned in 1916 as an extension lecturer at Hartford Theological Seminary, and spent 1917–1919 again in the Far East. During these years there were gradually forming in his mind the principles of Christian work with individuals which he felt the world most needed. A letter written at that time states clearly his purpose : " This principle [of personalised evangelism] is the essential of all Christianity and the absolute essential of all progress. The depersonalisation of all activity is one of the great problems of our day. In business, education, and in every mission activity we must return to this fundamental principle of Christ as a constant, and get into touch with men individually. Those whom we long to win must be in touch with the soul of the movement, which is any human heart aflame with the vital fire."

It was a youthful fellow-passenger across the Pacific in 1917 who was the means of crystallising certain principles of action which since have formed the basis of his work. She had heard him refer to normal Christianity as enabling the ordinary person to do the extraordinary thing, and asked one evening how an ordinary person like herself could win others to Christ. "But," she cautioned, "if you tell me, you must tell me very simply." In his "quiet time" next morning these five words came, and he wrote them down —Confidence, Confession, Conviction, Conversion, Continuance.

The first is the natural development of friendly acquaintance. The second is the normal result of intimate friendship, when barriers are levelled and each sees the other as he is. The third, conviction of sin, is the normal result of the impact upon a man of a quality of life which he instinctively knows to be superior to his own, the lack of which he recognises as an offence against God, and as his fault and only his. Conversion is the radical change of values brought about by God's Spirit working in the heart.

Continuance is that life-long process of growth familiar both to religion and to psychology. In the realm of religion it involves personal discipline— prayer, Bible study, times of quiet for listening to the direction of the Holy Spirit ; and it involves personal witness, conveying to others what conversion to Christ has meant to one's self. In the realm of psychology it involves an outlet in intelligent expressional activity for the emotion which otherwise would either die or show itself in undesirable ways.

There is a further point involved in the principle of Continuance which I feel is a unique contribution to the religious life of to-day. This is the principle of training leadership to carry on the work, not as a loose confederation of units, but as a body of men going forward, as they did after Pentecost, " with one heart and mind." It is a principle which takes pains and time. It means laying one's life alongside another's and staying by him until he is not only changed himself, but able under God to change others, and until he is willing to work in harmony with those engaged in like tasks.

Four friends[1] of Mr. Buchman occur to me as illustrating this principle—three Americans and a Scotsman. They are all college graduates, and could have had the best the world affords had they so desired. What is more, they craved it in one form or another until the day when they met a man who asked them to forsake all for Christ.

[1] " Persona Grata," " The Virginian," " Beau Ideal " in *Life Changers*; and " The Militant Mystic " in *Twice-Born Ministers*, by S. M. Shoemaker, Jr. [Revell, 1929.]

They had met less radical challenges, with which
they had toyed or which they had ignored. This
idea caught their imagination. It was new. It
was startling. It was presumptuous. But it gave
them pause. Then, month by month, as they saw
more and more of this interesting person—sometimes travelling, sometimes resting, but constantly
in touch with human problems, constantly amazed
at the miracles of regeneration which took place,
seeing more and more how they themselves could
be used to like ends—gradually there unfolded
within them a picture of what they might do for the
world were they to give their *all*.

It would have been so easy for any one of these
four to have filled his conventional niche in the
business or professional or religious world. But it
was not such a spirit that once turned the world
upside down.

IV

During the years immediately following the war,
the conviction grew on Mr. Buchman that the most
neglected and ill-handled field of spiritual endeavour
in the English-speaking world was to be found in the
colleges and universities of Britain and America.
He saw, too, that there was no group of people better
able to bring about a vital Christian movement.
They were young, intelligent, cultured, but, for most
of them conventional religion was at best a burden
to be endured, and at worst a myth to be ignored.
To awaken interest something distinctive was
needed. The week-end house-party, an established

channel of social intercourse, offered an evident solution of the problem.

In the summer of 1918 the first house-party took place at Kuling, a Central China summer resort, with a group of about a hundred Chinese and foreign Christians—missionaries, pastors, statesmen, business and professional men. They were together for two weeks, talking about the deepest things in their own experiences, acknowledging frankly where life had been a failure, and seeking to find whether it held more in store for them than they had already found.

Two years later Buchman was in Cambridge, England, with letters to sons of a number of men he had met in the Far East. Two young Englishmen returned with him to visit certain colleges in the United States, and the next summer (1921) there was held in Cambridge a week-end group for university men from both Oxford and Cambridge. A Member of Parliament, who was present, set the tone of the gathering by frankly acknowledging that he had spent his life seeking things for himself, that he was dissatisfied, unhappy, that he wished the young men present to profit by his mistakes. Harold Begbie, widely known journalist and author, attended a similar house-party later on as a rather critical observer, but was so impressed by the phenomenal change in certain individuals over the week-end that he went to Frank Buchman and asked permission to write a book about his work. The latter consented, provided no mention were made of his own name, and the book, entitled *Life Changers* (" More Twice-Born Men ") was subsequently published both in this country and in England.

Since then there has been a growing number of house-parties in both England and America.[1] The name has held because it best describes the atmosphere of these gatherings, which in their general setting more closely resemble a secular house-party than the usual religious " conference " or " convention." E. S. Martin has called them " the church in the house." They range in size from twenty to a hundred and fifty or more. The place is a country inn, a hotel, or private residence, according to the demand for space. The period of time extends from a week-end to a week or ten days. Youth in the twenties is more in evidence than age, but there are now a growing number of parents, teachers, and older people who come, and have learned that a searching Christian experience is no prerogative of the younger generation. Professions represented are apt to run all the way from selling newspapers and bootlegging to presiding over schools and theological seminaries. Younger business men and their wives, college undergraduates, society girls, and stenographers make up the balance.

Groups are held in the living-room, and people are free to come or go as they choose. Informality is the order of the day. The basis of invitation is friendship, and this, together with the times when simple introductions are in order, makes for a relationship among those present that is warm and personal.

The object of the house-party is frankly to relate modern individuals to Jesus Christ in terms which they understand and in an environment which they

[1] And recently, through the original interest of a Rhodes Scholar and Oxford boxing captain, in South Africa.

find congenial. The fundamentals of the Christian message are covered in a series of informal talks on Sin, Surrender, Conversion, Guidance, and the rationale of intelligent Witness, or how to convey to another one's own experience of Christ. Bible study usually takes up an important part of each day. Separate groups for men and women, often divided as to age and profession, provide an opportunity for discussion of various problems connected with sex or money or life work in a more intimate vein than is possible in a mixed gathering. Each morning opens with a time of united quiet, during which thought is directed toward God in full conviction that, to a mind and heart eager to discover it, He can make known His will. The evenings provide a period when anyone can talk who wants to.

A bishop of the Episcopal Church who attended a house-party last June has noted down some of his impressions as follows :—

"The Minnewaska house-party, June 21–28, was a revelation to me. It revealed a kind of vitality which seems to me the fundamental need of the Church and of individual Christians, men and women, to-day. The good fellowship was striking, for it appeared not simply in fun and good times, but seemed to go to the very bottom of the deepest things we know or hope or fear. The emphasis upon the possibility and need of daily, indeed constant, communion with God, and guidance by His Spirit, echoed the many-sided appeal of St. Paul ' to the saints that are in Christ.'

" Sin was dealt with in the frank and direct way which youth demands. Nothing was glossed over, yet there was no morbidity. Chief attention, in the public meetings, was given to those sins of envy, pride, censoriousness, cowardice, sloth, uncharitableness, and insincerity which are so often fatal to fellowship and spiritual vigour just because they are not recognised as equally serious with the gross and carnal sins. The aseptic atmosphere of these discussions owed much to the fact that the ludicrous stupidity of many sins shone out vividly in obviously sincere confession, and brought out spontaneously the cleansing laughter of the whole group.

"Frequent reference was made to the need of discipline, beginning with the regular observance of the morning watch or time of quiet, but refusing to stop short of whatever is required to bring us up to our *best* in body, mind, spirit, and social relationships.

"Most significant of all, I think, was the group life there described, and for a few days lived out by a large proportion of those present. 'Sharing,' or manifest willingness to 'share' to the limit, was at work before our eyes, and through it the Holy Spirit was giving courage to the timid, hope to those on the verge of despair, insight to the blind, in some cases life out of spiritual death, and initiating all who were willing to the hope and joy and strength that come from creative experience in the moral and spiritual realm."

V

Most people to-day are facing two problems—sex and money. These house-party groups, I believe, are helping to solve them.

The question of sex needs no emphasis to bring it into the open. It is already emphasised, not to say over-emphasised, in literature, moving pictures, and social relationships, with a freedom unheard-of for over a century. Psychiatrists say that it is an important factor in a great majority of their cases. Doctors state that in some form or other it is a nearly universal problem with both men and women. Every minister who deals searchingly with any form of the confessional knows that he cannot avoid meeting it. Yet the attitude of most parents, teachers, and Churches toward this problem in all its perplexing ramifications is marked by timidity and clumsiness. Sex is discussed nowadays in nearly every conceivable atmosphere but that in which it is most likely to find a solution, namely, an atmosphere dedicated to Jesus Christ.

This group of people, in the first place, recognise the sex problem as one that exists. What some call sexual experimentation they would call sin. In the second place, they recognise that the instinct is at bottom a God-given one, and, while they do not condone any perversion of thought or word or deed, they know that the real problem is not one of suppression, but one of control and sublimation. As in the case of other problems, they believe that the cure lies ultimately, not in mere human force of will, but in the cleansing stream of spiritual life that follows upon a genuine conversion. It is what St. Paul means when he writes, " Walk in the Spirit, and ye shall not fulfil the lust of the flesh." It is what a great psychologist has called " the expulsive power of a higher affection."

It is, of course, not a subject for discussion in mixed groups. In separate groups for men and women it is not infrequently brought up, and real help afforded by a frank and aseptic canvassing of various aspects of the problem, including the problems of marriage and divorce. In dealing with individuals it is considered advisable to be alert to its manifestations, to be ready, if necessary, to discuss it very personally and very frankly, and always to indicate that the only adequate solution comes from God, whose renewing moral power flows into the life of one who wholly surrenders to His will as revealed in Jesus Christ.

Then there is the problem of money and possessions, with its related problem of social injustice. This is the crux of the Communist hatred of Christianity, and is the chief reason why one sees over against the Chapel of the Iberian Virgin in Moscow the Russian motto, " Religion is the opium of the people." It must be faced by anyone or any group that wishes to commend the gospel of Christ to our modern world.

Much is to be said for the Communist ideal—from each according to his ability, to each according to his need. Something like this state *ought* to exist, but it doesn't. The problem is what to do about it.

It is in his method of solution that the Marxian Communist takes issue with the follower of Christ. Michael Borodin, two years ago the dominant figure in South China and chief Soviet adviser to the Nationalist Government, once told me in his picturesque way what he considered the chief difference between pure Communism and pure Christianity. " You," he said, " undertake to bring in the Kingdom of God through love. We are striving to bring it in by force."

The members of this group of which I have been speaking accept this challenge. They sympathise with efforts to remedy economic ills by legislation and to awaken a more sensitive social conscience. They realise, too, that these, like the Communist

appeal to armed force, are not final solutions, because
they seek to mould men's conduct in one area without sufficient reference to man's primary need in
every area, which is God. They are palliatives, not
cures.

Jesus appears in a sense to have chosen between
social leadership and spiritual leadership. He recognised that the problem at bottom was an individual
one. What counted first of all was not environment,
but character. He can be said to have founded the
" social gospel " only in so far as this is derived
from a radical application of the personal gospel.
So I feel that this group is true to what was most
distinctive in Christ's method when it lays its main
emphasis, not on modifying men's actions, but on
changing men's lives.

The truth of this assumption—that, once given
this thorough change of life, its social implications will eventually follow—is illustrated by the
story of a certain Scotsman, head of a printing plant
in the Orient. Contemptuous of all religion, he
had for many years resisted every attempt to reform
either himself or his business. A mutual friend gave
Buchman a card of introduction. Two days of
tactful handling brought this hardened executive
to his knees before God. Instantly his personal life
changed. Drinking and gambling were among the
first to go. Then he didn't lose his temper when an
office-boy forgot to get some important letters into
the home mail. Then he began to be considerate
to his chauffeur—had he had his breakfast when
called early in the morning ? Each day new areas
became clear. Nothing had been said about labour

conditions, but one morning he called in his native foremen. "You men," he said, "have worked because you feared me. That's all wrong. From now on Christ is the head of this business, and all of us must help." He pointed to the nearest Indian. "I lost my temper with you this morning. I want to apologise. . . . " The next step was to put everyone of his three hundred employees on a living wage.

Money and possessions are treated by the group as belonging to that whole category of material things which are not in themselves either evil or good, which are given for our use, but which, in proportion as our desire for them overrides our desire for God, can effectually keep God out. In so far as they do this they are a cause of sin, and must be dealt with like any other sin. In a word, they must be "surrendered." To a man sincerely trying to do God's will rather than his own, and seeking daily guidance toward this end, there is no problem either of pride in receiving for his own needs or of miserliness in giving to supply the needs of others. There results a form of practical sharing of possessions which seems to me to hold the germ of a truly spiritual solution for the problem of material inequality. There results, too, a literal casting of all *anxious* concern, for the world and for the individual, upon God, with a resolve to give to the limit whenever guided to do so, but not to worry in general where one cannot help in particular. They, and all they have, belong to their fellowmen, but only because first of all they belong to God.

VI

I am reminded of a reflection attributed to Goethe —" Truth can never be expressed ; Truth can only be lived." After all, the unit of interest, like the ultimate unit of value, will be the individual life. Nothing that lacks capacity for radically altering lives is likely to stir, still less to unify, the Churches, nations, and races of the world. Conversely, whatever proves its power over the individual holds implications for the mass—"a programme of life," as Mr. Buchman puts it, "which issues in personal, social, national, and international salvation." I am convinced that nothing short of a coalition of individual spiritual regenerations will serve to produce that corporate spiritual regenerationwhich we so need.

Now an individual spiritual regeneration need not be spectacular. Occasionally it is. It was spectacular when a veteran bootlegger in an Eastern city recently found Christ and started out to vend his discovery in place of his liquor. It was spectacular when a still youthful son of privilege from the South, versed for ten years in the more sordid ways of the world, changed his course and decided on the ministry. It was spectacular when his own experience, shared with a college graduate in an hour oi need, proved the medium for a cure which had been beyond the power of psychiatry. But even more impressive, it seems to me, is the experience of a young New York business man[1] and his wife who found in Christianity lived to the hilt a joy they had

[1] "In Spite of Himself," in *Children of the Second Birth*, by S. M. Shoemaker, Jr. (Revell, 1927).

vainly sought in the glamour of their own social set. We are reasonably well accustomed to the conversion of a "down-and-outer." His need is obvious. When vital religion lays hold on an "up-and-outer" —one of that growing body of pleasant pagans who apparently have all they want in this world and the next—it is time for the professional Christian to be concerned. Something explosive is on foot.

I am told they were the last people one would naturally consider as candidates for conversion. Till two years ago their lives were like the lives of hundreds of other young couples scattered over our broad land. He was a popular member of his class at an aristocratic Eastern university. She was a sought-after débutante in New York a few seasons ago. Together they went everywhere and did everything. Life rested lightly on their shoulders. They were lovable, attractive, unselfish in a self-centred sort of way, approved religion, and attended church in so far as this was done. To them might have been applied literally the remark of Dr. Alexander Whyte of Scotland about his own generation— that they had every virtue but a sense of sin.

I asked him for an autobiographical sketch up to date, and this is the result : —

From 1913 to 1925 I managed a complete spiritual vacation while accomplishing prep. school, college, four years of business, and, in 1924, an exceedingly happy marriage. I had been raised on the customary Presbyterian Sunday-school diet, and graduated into prep. school with well-defined notions about religion and God. My beliefs were that religion was bounded on all sides by the duty of obeying the Ten Commandments, that God was a combination of school-teacher and policeman, and that if you obeyed the Commandments fairly well He would let you alone. I began then to live without Him. Nothing terrible happened, so I proceeded to forget about Him except when I was in trouble.

I had managed to retain from the boy stage a fairly clean way of life, a high sense of duty toward civilisation in general, and a desire to help others—all of which were based on family pride, Mother and Dad having instilled into me the firm belief that people who were anybody showed it by the fact of their desire to help others, and by setting an example that would be a little above their environment. I, personally, thought I had a lot to give to other people, and that I could make their lives work out better if they would only ask my advice. No one did ask, however, so I had no chance to find out how useless I was on the deeper levels.

My wife and I thought it was the thing for representative younger married couples in New York to have a church connection, and, from many which we tried out, we selected Calvary Episcopal because we found there a younger crowd of people enthusiastic about something. What our life lacked was a joint enthusiasm for something bigger than ourselves, so we started to try to find what seemed to give these Calvary people such a zest in living. They made a natural humorous crowd from all walks and stations of life, but they all seemed to have a definite purpose in view. To my real-estate-broker mind, each one seemed to have a big deal on.

We became more and more interested. But I had entered in as an equal with these people, and I found by the contrast of our lives, as the year went by, that I was not even born spiritually, whereas they were actively growing up. It took many months for my imagination to be sufficiently developed to see clearly a quality of life which was miles above ours. An entirely new picture of sin became clear to me, and many things in my life showed the necessity of being weeded out, not because they were bad in the world's sense, but because they stood in the way of my drawing closer to God and to the people around me. Among these

was my independent attitude towards God—leaving Him
out of my whole daily scheme of thought and never asking
Him to make plans for my life.

It might be remarked at this point that most
people have a distorted notion of just what constitutes sin. Most of us would concede that murder
and theft and adultery were sins. Many would be
inclined to include lying. Some would add bad
temper. Few would be likely to give the definition
which is implied throughout the Gospels—that,
fundamentally, sin is independence toward God.
Most of us incline to take a passive and negative view
of sin as transgression of an ethical code. Jesus
went deeper, and placed the emphasis on an active
and positive quality of life : " Thou shalt love the
Lord thy God with all thy heart . . . [and] thy
neighbour as thyself." Not so much by what
a man does as by what he leaves undone will he be
judged. The criterion is Christlikeness. It would
have been hard to convict this young business man
on the basis of the Ten Commandments. What did
convict him was a power in others which he coveted
for himself. He felt no sense of need until he realised
that he had nothing but impotent sympathy for a
friend in need. That lack he had to recognise as sin.

Soon after this, at the conclusion of an evening
group which met weekly in an up-town apartment,
he slipped away with one[1] of the four men referred
to earlier in this article. Sitting there on a sofa,
shortly before midnight, God flooded into his life.
Two weeks later his wife joined him in this new
experience.

[1] " Persona Grata," in *Life Changers*.

It is commonly stated that religion would be all right were it only practical. I recall in this connection the distinction drawn by a biographer of St. Francis of Assisi between a practical life and one that is merely " immediately practicable." Our business friend's conclusion follows :—

Difficulties very soon arose in my business because I did not want to let this field into the new scheme of things. It is difficult to turn over your life completely on a basis of faith ; and I decided that God could run my social relationships, but that my wife and I would probably starve if I let Him into my business affairs. I dreaded being thought an impractical idealist. So I kept very quiet around the office about religious matters. This was unnatural and double-faced, and therefore uncomfortable. But certain questions had to be faced and decided because God seemed to want me to stay in business. If I was to control the making of money, could I let God have control over the spending of it ? And the question arose of what to do about time taken out of business hours for guided spiritual contacts, of God's time crossing my time, of money spent or given away under guidance in amounts that I did not seem able to afford humanly, of what to tell the office people about the times when I disappeared from my desk for an afternoon or an hour, of the question of office allegiance and duty to my employer. It had to be one of two ways—God to have all or nothing. Finally I took the full plunge, surrendered to God my desire for business success, my fear of needing money, my cherished reputation as a hard-headed, practical person, and decided to let Him have His way in all things. Immediately the fears were solved, and business people turned out to be just like everyone anywhere. Where I did not fear the individuals, contacts have become real, business affairs go far better in less time, and the relationship of time spent on different things is now solved because all time belongs to God.

God makes a difference. The step which these

two people took shows not alone in a serenity of look and thought and action, and in a quiet joy which the world may ruffle, but which it cannot disturb. It has shown itself also in its direct effect on others. In a little book published some forty years ago, entitled *Modern Christianity : A Civilised Heathenism*, a cultured Parsee enquires of a worldly Anglican divine just what difference exists between a nominal believer and a high-minded unbeliever. And he continues with this challenge : " If the age of miracles has ceased, it must be because the age of personal witness has begun. Never yet was a man asked to believe in a supernatural God without evidence supernatural. This is the evidence which I demand." This demand for evidence is one which the world has a perfect right to make of a Church and of people who claim to have found something worth spreading. It is the scientific attitude. It is the judicial attitude. It was Christ's attitude— " By their fruits ye shall know them."

His wife's sister had married a banker in a large Eastern city. This man had attended church in childhood through family custom. He continued at school because of compulsory chapel. The years at university, where he led a gay life, offered more freedom, but only business brought release from that routine religion which so thoroughly bored him. After marriage, his wife took him for a while to Sunday services. That soon went. A few business friends kept it up ; but, he argued, they behaved just like himself, and, if Christianity made no visible difference, why go to church at all? Shortly afterwards grace before meals was dropped, " Because," he explains, "it just didn't seem to mix with cocktails."

One summer this couple visited Europe, leaving their little girl, aged ten, with the sister and brother-in-law. The child saw her aunt keeping quiet times before breakfast, and before long appeared with a small notebook, announcing that she, too, was going to "listen to God." Her parents on their return became interested enough in their daughter's experiment to attend a house-party. The husband, expecting to be bored again, and irritated at having to miss the mid-winter ball, came fortified with a bottle of Scotch and a novel. Intrigued by the company, he stayed, and tried a quiet time. Three thoughts occurred. Hesitantly he committed them to the back of an envelope—" Be frank to admit that God is all-powerful "; " Material things : what do they matter ? "; " The peace that passeth understanding."

He turned to a young minister [1] whom he had known at college, and whose work in a New York city parish he greatly admired : " Would you call that *guidance* ? "

The man smiled. " What do *you* think ? What are your real problems ? "

Musingly he replied : " Spending too much money and ' keeping up with the Joneses.' " From that moment, he tells me, and for the first time in his life, he began really to think.

There followed during the next few weeks one of those contagious transformations that make one sure the age of miracles did not die with the apostles.

[1] " The Virginian," in *Life Changers*.

The home life is different. Formerly, he says, he had come to regard the children as so much furniture. Now family prayers, ending with a time of quiet followed by sharing of guidance, is a daily necessity before business. Petty irritations at the office no longer provoke. Not long ago fifty of their summer social set dropped in during polo week to discuss personal religion. Drink, suicide, divorce, bereavement—he and his wife have dealt successfully with them all in the lives of others. They are influencing for Christ a section of society with which the forces of organised religion have almost completely lost touch. The bishop—for they have returned to their Church—has since referred to the husband as his most spiritually influential layman.

I could gather the stories of a hundred or two hundred people on both sides of the Atlantic whose lives have been as radically and fruitfully changed. They come from all walks of life and are of all ages, although the majority are young men and women. They do not represent any unique dispensation of the Spirit. They bear witness to that dispensation which has been abroad in the world ever since Christ died. Only they have received it in terms of their own generation, and they tell of it in the language of to-day.

Throughout the English-speaking world and beyond—in churches, in homes, in offices—little groups are meeting to conserve, strengthen, and transmit to others their new-found secret. It is indeed an open secret. But to each one it comes as a fresh and luminous discovery. Do not be surprised to hear them speak of this " way " with the disturbing authority of first-hand experience, and in full conviction that it is available to all.   It was a distinguished philosopher who wrote, commenting on a certain " divine right " implied in the apostolic message,   " Historically   speaking,   the   crux   of Christianity is its element of presumption."   These people have found what is a very rare thing in this modern world—a core of inward spiritual certainty. They have, not a question, but an answer.

By HAROLD BEGBIE

PUNISHMENT AND PERSONALITY

Crown 8vo.   **5s.** net.

Church Times.—"One cannot read this book without admiration. In the survey of our prisons he observes so carefully and reports what he has seen so vividly that it is hard to stop reading him."

Lancet.—"Contains a great deal of information sanely put ; a real sympathy for the prisoners is never made doubtful by any sentimentality, and the character sketches of the inmates and their guardians, from the governor downwards, are drawn with a thoroughly observant pen. A well balanced essay."

BROKEN LIGHTS

A short study in the varieties of Christian Opinion

Popular Edition.   Crown 8vo.   **2s. 6d.** net

"Broken Lights " is an attempt on the part of the Author to think himself into the minds of various believers, and to present in simple language and with convenient brevity the opinions which they hold with obvious devotion, those conflicting opinions which make one man a Roman Catholic ; another an Anglo-Catholic ; one man a Conservative Modernist, another a Liberal Evangelical ; one man a Quaker, another a Unitarian.

A LONDON GIRL   1s. 6d. net.

The BISHOP OF LONDON, addressing a meeting at the Northampton Institute, Finsbury, said : "I have lately been reading a story which interested and impressed me very much indeed. All you men ought to read it. It was called 'A London Girl.' The picture painted in it made a great impression on me, because I know from my own experience in rescue and preventive work that the story is literally true. It is the story of the downfall of hundreds of our girls in London to-day. The pitiful tale is not overdrawn ; it is all too true."

LIFE WITHOUT SERVANTS

The Rediscovery of Domestic Happiness

By A SURVIVOR (Harold Begbie)

New edition with an introduction and footnotes by CHARLES E. HECHT.

Foolscap 8vo.   **2s. 6d.** net.

Lady.—"Full of mellow wisdom and practical suggestions."

By A GENTLEMAN WITH A DUSTER

(HAROLD BEGBIE)

FICTION

PLAIN SAILING

Fourteenth Thousand **2s. 6d.** net.

Yorkshire Post.—" Will linger in the reader's mind."
Truth.—" Extremely well told and well written."
Glasgow Herald.—" Enjoyable and meritorious."
Daily Sketch.—" Has beauty and strength."

THE LASLETT AFFAIR

Fifth Edition. **2s. 6d.** net.

Spectator.—" It is vigorously written and presents a great variety of true scenes of modern English life as well as many of those penetrating reflections on social and religious matters in which this gifted writer always excels."

JULIUS LEVINE

Sixth Edition. **2s. 6d.** net.

Spectator.—" The story has a good and sometimes exciting plot. But its great charm lies in its wealth of characteristically English scenes and portraits, and in its incidental reflections on contemporary problems and manners."

THE OTHER DOOR

Sixth Edition. **2s. 6d.** net.

Punch.—" A book to which six writers out of seven would have been glad to put their names. ' The Other Door ' is a stimulating and thought-provoking book and good enough, even as a story, to go on everyone's library list. May the gentleman continue ! "

By A GENTLEMAN WITH A DUSTER

(HAROLD BEGBIE)

NON-FICTION

POMPS AND VANITIES
Popular Edition. Crown 8vo. **2s. 6d.** net.
A direct challenge to the whole thesis of materialism, and explains why both religion and philosophy in all ages have so earnestly condemned " the world."

THE HOWLING MOB : An Indictment of Democracy
Popular Edition. Crown 8vo. **2s. 6d.** net.
Sunday Times.—" A very clever and brilliantly written book."

DECLENSION
Popular Edition. Crown 8vo. **2s. 6d.** net.
Birmingham Post.—" ' The Gentleman with a Duster ' has written a thoughtful and, we might say, a passionate book."

THE CONSERVATIVE MIND
Popular Edition. Crown 8vo. **2s. 6d.** net.
Aberdeen Press.—" ' The Conservative Mind ' stands out with convincing clarity as embodying a policy that alone offers a genuine alternative to the Socialistic mind."

SEVEN AGES : A Narrative of the Human Mind
Popular Edition. Crown 8vo. **2s. 6d.** net.
Cambridge Review.—" Never controversial, always sympathetic —a treasure house of happy phrases, almost epigrammatic in their brevity and truth."

THE GLASS OF FASHION : Some Social Reflections
Popular Edition. Crown 8vo. **2s. 6d.** net.
Spectator.—" . . . he is destined to light a match which in the future may be used to light a candle that will illuminate our little corner of the world."

PAINTED WINDOWS : A Study in Religious Personality
Popular Edition. Crown 8vo. **2s. 6d.** net.
Daily Graphic.—" A new book which will rank, for satiric wit, for trenchant and not unfair criticism, and for vivid portraiture, with his ' Mirrors of Downing Street.' "

ABOUT HEALING-HABITS

The classic spiritual texts republished by healing-habits represent the rebirth of important books that had a significant impact on the lives of the people of yesteryear. This is our humble attempt to contribute, in a small way, to the healing and recovery of people who are today suffering from any malady of the body, mind, or spirit. The saving of even one life makes our republishing worthwhile.

BOOKS REPUBLISHED BY HEALING-HABITS:

When Man Listens: Everyone Can Listen to God
by Cecil Rose; republished by Tuchy Palmieri
(BookSurge, 2008)

The Genius of Fellowship – Originally titled, **The
Conversion of the Church**
by Samuel M. Shoemaker; republished by Tuchy Palmieri
(BookSurge, 2008)

Life Changers: 13th Edition
by Harold Begbie; republished by Tuchy Palmieri
(BookSurge, 2009)

Twice Born Ministers: We Are All Ministers
by Samuel M. Shoemaker; republished by Tuchy Palmieri
(BookSurge, 2009)

Children of the Second Birth
by Samuel M. Shoemaker; republished by Tuchy Palmieri
(BookSurge, 2009)

Twice Born Men: A Clinic of Regeneration
by Harold Begbie; republished by Tuchy Palmieri
(BookSurge, 2009)

ALSO BY CARL "TUCHY" PALMIERI – BOOKS ON RECOVERY

The Platinum Rule and Other Contrarian Sayings: The First 60 Years
(BookSurge, 2006)

Tuchy's Law and Other Contrarian Quotes To Help You In Life's Journey
(BookSurge, 2007)

Off The Wall Contrarian Quotes For People In Recovery
(BookSurge, 2007)

The Food Contrarian: Quotes for People Recovering From or Dealing With Eating Issues
(BookSurge, 2007)

Relationship Recovery: Healing One Relationship At A Time
(BookSurge, 2008)

ALSO BY CARL "TUCHY" PALMIERI – INSPIRATIONAL BOOKS

The Godsons: The Trinity Alliance
(BookSurge, 2007)

Josephine, In Her Words: Our Mom
(BookSurge, 2007)

Phil, In His Words: Our Dad
(BookSurge, 2007)

Relationship Magic
(BookSurge, 2008)

Money And So Much More: The True Meaning of Wealth
(BookSurge, 2008)

Sex and Intimacy: The Gifts of Life
(BookSurge, 2008)

Oprah, In Her Words: Our American Princess
(BookSurge, 2008)

Satisfying Success: And the Ways to Achieve It
(BookSurge, 2009)

Obama, In His Own Words: Pre-Election
(BookSurge, 2009)

ABOUT THE AUTHOR

Carl "Tuchy" Palmieri was born in 1942 in an old mansion belonging to the former mill owner of the factory where his father worked. His family was one of six related families that occupied the mansion. The second son of Italian immigrants, Carl grew up in Westport, Connecticut. After receiving a bachelor's degree in business administration from the University of Bridgeport he began his career marketing and installing accounting computers for the Burroughs Corporation. Twenty-one years later, in 1987, he started his own computer business. Carl is also the author of a series of self-help books.

Today Carl lives with his wife, Susan, in Fairfield, Connecticut. He has three children, two stepchildren, and 12 grandchildren. His nickname, Tuchy, comes from having been one of three Carls in his family. There was a "Big Carl," a "Carl the Twin," and "Carluch," which meant "Little Carl." "Carluch" evolved into "Carlatuch," "Tuch," and finally, "Tuchy."

Printed in Great Britain
by Amazon

62553199R00117